RELIGIONS OF AFRICA

MASON CREST
PHILADELPHIA

RELIGIONS OF AFRICA

Lora Friedenthal and Dorothy Kavanaugh

MASON CREST
PHILADELPHIA

Frontispiece: African Christians pray during a church service. Most Africans identify themselves as followers of one of three religious systems: Christianity, Islam, or an indigenous tribal religion.

Mason Crest
450 Parkway Drive, Suite D
Broomall, PA 19008
www.masoncrest.com

© 2014 by Mason Crest, an imprint of National Highlights, Inc.

Printed and bound in the United States of America.

CPSIA Compliance Information: Batch #APP2013. For further information, contact Mason Crest at 1-866-MCP-Book

First printing
1 3 5 7 9 8 6 4 2

Library of Congress Cataloging-in-Publication Data

Friedenthal, Lora.
  Religions of Africa / Lora Friedenthal and Dorothy Kavanaugh.
     p. cm. — (Africa: progress and problems)
  Includes bibliographical references and index.
  ISBN 978-1-4222-2947-7 (hc)
  ISBN 978-1-4222-8892-4 (ebook)
  1. Africa—Religion—Juvenile literature.
  I. Kavanaugh, Dorothy, 1969- II. Title. III. Series: Africa, progress & problems.
  BL2400.F69 2013
  200.96—dc23

                                    2013013036

Africa: Progress and Problems series ISBN: 978-1-4222-2934-7

Table of Contents

AFRICA: PROGRESS AND PROBLEMS

THE PROMISE OF TODAY'S AFRICA

by Robert I. Rotberg

Today's Africa is a mosaic of effective democracy and desperate despotism, immense wealth and abysmal poverty, conscious modernity and mired traditionalism, bitter conflict and vast arenas of peace, and enormous promise and abiding failure. Generalizations are more difficult to apply to Africa or Africans than elsewhere. The continent, especially the sub-Saharan two-thirds of its immense landmass, presents enormous physical, political, and human variety. From snow-capped peaks to intricate patches of remaining jungle, from desolate deserts to the greatest rivers, and from the highest coastal sand dunes anywhere to teeming urban conglomerations, Africa must be appreciated from myriad perspectives. Likewise, its peoples come in every shape and size, govern themselves in several complicated manners, worship a host of indigenous and imported gods, and speak thousands of original and five or six derivative common languages. To know Africa is to know nuance and complexity.

There are 54 nation-states that belong to the African Union, 49 of which are situated within the sub-Saharan mainland or on its offshore islands. No other continent has so many countries, political divisions, or members of the General Assembly of the United Nations. No other continent encompasses so many

distinctively different peoples or spans such geographical disparity. On no other continent have so many innocent civilians
lost their lives in intractable civil wars—15 million since 1991
in such places as Algeria, Angola, the Congo, Côte d'Ivoire,
Liberia, Sierra Leone, and Sudan. No other continent has so
many disparate natural resources (from cadmium, cobalt, and
copper to petroleum and zinc) and so little to show for their
frenzied exploitation. No other continent has proportionally so
many people subsisting (or trying to) on less than $2 a day. But
then no other continent has been so beset by HIV/AIDS (30
percent of all adults in southern Africa), by tuberculosis, by
malaria (prevalent almost everywhere), and by less well-known
scourges such as schistosomiasis (liver fluke), several kinds of
filariasis, river blindness, trachoma, and trypanosomiasis
(sleeping sickness).

Africa is among the most Christian continents, but it also is
home to more Muslims than the Middle East. Apostolic and
Pentecostal churches are immensely powerful. So are Sufi
brotherhoods. Yet traditional African religions are still influential. So is a belief in spirits and witches (even among
Christians and Muslims), in faith healing and in alternative
medicine. Polygamy remains popular. So does the practice of
female circumcision and other long-standing cultural prefer-
ences. Africa cannot be well understood without appreciating
how village life still permeates the great cities and how urban
pursuits engulf villages. Africa can no longer be considered
predominantly rural, agricultural, or wild; more than half of
its peoples live in towns and cities.

Political leaders must cater to both worlds, old and new.
They and their followers must join the globalized, Internet-

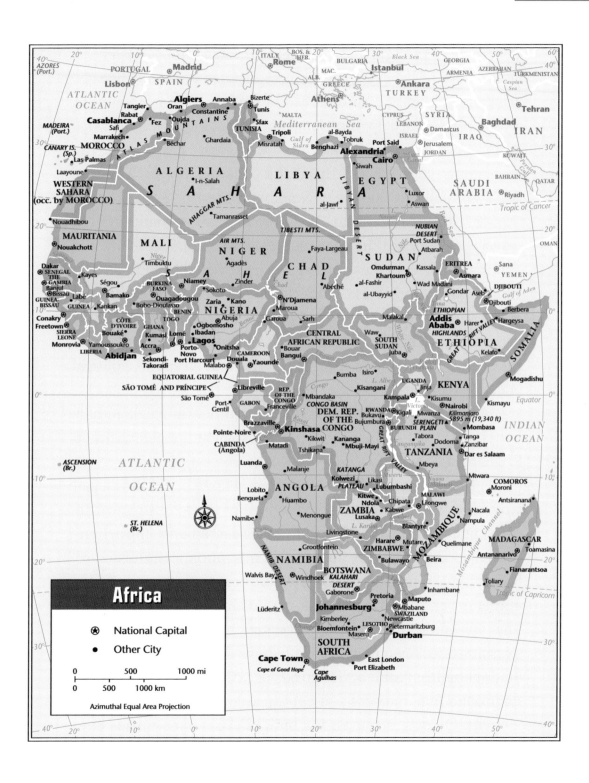

Africa

⊛ National Capital

• Other City

0   500   1000 mi

0   500   1000 km

Azimuthal Equal Area Projection

penetrated world even as they remain rooted appropriately in past modes of behavior, obedient to dictates of family, lineage, tribe, and ethnicity. This duality often results in democracy or at least partially participatory democracy. Equally often it develops into autocracy. Botswana and Mauritius have enduring democratic governments. In Benin, Ghana, Kenya, Lesotho, Malawi, Mali, Mozambique, Namibia, Nigeria, Senegal, South Africa, Tanzania, and Zambia fully democratic pursuits are relatively recent and not yet sustainably implanted. Algeria, Cameroon, Chad, the Central African Republic, Egypt, the Sudan, and Tunisia are authoritarian entities run by strongmen. Zimbabweans and Equatorial Guineans suffer from even more venal rule. Swazis and Moroccans are subject to the real whims of monarchs. Within even this vast sweep of political practice there are still more distinctions. The partial democracies represent a spectrum. So does the manner in which authority is wielded by kings, by generals, and by long-entrenched civilian autocrats.

The democratic countries are by and large better developed and more rapidly growing economically than those ruled by strongmen. In Africa there is an association between the pursuit of good governance and beneficial economic performance. Likewise, the natural resource wealth curse that has afflicted mineral-rich countries such as the Congo and Nigeria has had the opposite effect in well-governed places like Botswana. Nation-states open to global trade have done better than those with closed economies. So have those countries with prudent managements, sensible fiscal arrangements, and modest deficits. Overall, however, the bulk of African countries have suffered in terms of reduced economic growth from the sheer fact of being tropical, beset by disease in an enervating climate where there is an average of one trained physician to every 13,000 persons. Many lose growth prospects, too, because of the absence of navigable rivers, the paucity of ocean and river ports, barely maintained roads, and few and narrow railroads. Moreover, 15 of Africa's countries are landlocked, without comfortable access to relatively inexpensive waterborne transport. Hence, imports and exports for much of Africa are more expensive than elsewhere as they move over formidable distances. Africa is the most underdeveloped continent because of geographical and health constraints that have not yet been overcome, because of ill-considered policies, because of the sheer number of separate nation-states (a colonial legacy), and because of poor governance.

Africa's promise is immense, and far more exciting than its achievements have been since a wave of nationalism and independence in the 1960s liberated nearly every section of the continent. Thus, the next several decades of the 21st century are ones of promise for Africa. The challenges are clear: to alleviate grinding poverty and deliver greater real economic goods to larger proportions of people in each country, and across all countries; to deliver more of the benefits of good governance to more of Africa's peoples; to end the destructive killing fields that run rampant across so much of Africa; to improve educational training and health services; and to roll back the scourges of HIV/AIDS, tuberculosis, and malaria. Every challenge represents an opportunity with concerted and bountiful Western assistance to transform the lives of Africa's vulnerable and resourceful future generations.

1 THE ROLE OF RELIGION IN AFRICA

At the dawn of the 21st century, religion continues to play a major role in shaping Africa both politically and socially. This is because, as the Kenyan theologian John Mbiti notes, "Africans are *notoriously* religious. . . . Religion permeates into all the departments of life so it is not easy or possible to isolate it [from other aspects of African society]." The famed South African church leader Archbishop Desmond Tutu made a similar comment: "It is religion, more than anything else, that colours [Africans'] understanding of the universe and their empirical participation in that universe, making life a profoundly religious phenomenon."

This attitude may seem strange to people living in the United States or other parts of the Western world, where there is often an imaginary "wall" separating religious beliefs from everyday life. But—speaking generally, of course—most Africans view religion as more than just a collection of teachings about how to

13

live a good, moral life. To Africans, religion is a way to resolve personal and social problems, such as illnesses, accidents, poverty, divorce, or the loss of a job. In their book *Worlds of Power: Religious Thought and Political Practice in Africa*, authors Stephen Ellis and Gerrie Ter Haar assert that the African religious revival over the past few decades is related to the continent's longstanding economic and political problems. "Africans look to religion both to understand and to overcome their current misfortunes," they write.

Africa is an enormous continent—the second largest in land area, after Asia—and contains a diverse population of more than 1 billion. Consequently, Africans practice all of the major world religions and hundreds of lesser-known faiths. However, the overwhelming majority of Africans—well over 98 percent of the population—identify themselves as followers of one of three religions: African Traditional Religion (ATR, the term

AFRICA'S OTHER RELIGIONS

A small percentage of Africans practice faiths other than the traditional religions, Christianity, or Islam. Some of these faiths have been rooted in Africa since ancient times, while others arrived during more recent periods of immigration to the continent.

Judaism established itself in North Africa before Christianity was born, and today small communities of Jews still exist in the Muslim North African countries, particularly Morocco, Tunisia, and Algeria. Since the establishment of Israel in 1948, the number of these communities has been greatly reduced as their members have immigrated to the Jewish state.

Elsewhere on the continent, there are a few significant Jewish communities. The Falasha are Jews who have lived in Ethiopia, a traditionally Christian country, for centuries. At one time there were more than 90,000 Falasha living in Ethiopia, but many have since immigrated to Israel; today, the African community numbers about 22,000. The Abayudaya are a small group of Jews who live in eastern Uganda. This sect was started by an African named Semei Kakungulu during the used for the multitude of indigenous religions observed on the continent), Christianity, or Islam. In a sense, all three of these religions can be considered indigenous to Africa. Although Christianity and Islam originally developed in the Middle East, both religions spread to Africa soon after their establishment.

Today, both Christianity and Islam are spreading rapidly throughout the continent. For example, Christianity is growing faster in Africa than in any other continent. Today, more than 470 million Christians live in sub-Saharan Africa, up from 117 million in 1970. There are more Christians living in Africa than there are in North America. The explosive growth of Christianity in Africa is largely due to evangelism. While the population of Muslims is not growing as quickly, more than 460 million Muslims live in Africa—about half of this number in sub-Saharan Africa. Only Asia has a larger Muslim population.

early 20th century. The Abayudaya survived persecutions under dictator Idi Amin (1971–79) and other Ugandan rulers, but the community remains quite small, numbering less than a thousand members. There is also a Jewish community of about 100,000 in South Africa, made up primarily of the descendants of immigrants from Lithuania during the 19th and early 20th centuries.

Another world religion, Hinduism, which is a primary faith of India, is found among Afro-Indian communities of eastern and southern Africa. The ancestors of these people were traders or merchants involved in the Indian Ocean trade. Hindus are the largest religious group in one African country, the island nation of Mauritius, where they make up about half of the population. Among Africans of Indian origin, there are also smaller communities whose members follow the South Asian religions Sikhism, Janism, and Parsi.

The continent of Africa is believed to contain the second-largest number of adherents to the Baha'i faith, which originated in Persia during the 19th century. Most Baha'i live in Asia (3.6 million); however, about 1.8 million are scattered throughout Africa. The center of Baha'i worship in Africa is a temple in Kampala, Uganda.

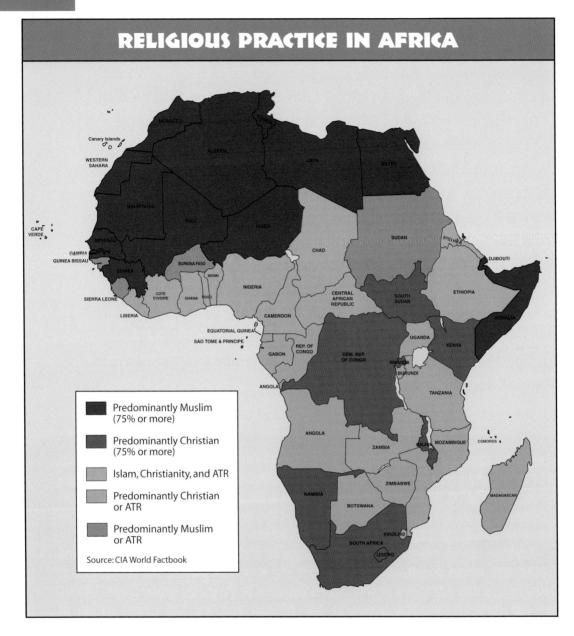

RELIGIOUS PRACTICE IN AFRICA

Predominantly Muslim (75% or more)

Predominantly Christian (75% or more)

Islam, Christianity, and ATR

Predominantly Christian or ATR

Predominantly Muslim or ATR

Source: CIA World Factbook

These statistics seem to indicate that the African Traditional Religion may eventually disappear. Indeed, the number of people identifying themselves as followers of an indigenous religion has dropped over the past four decades. However, these ancient indigenous religions are both adaptable (incorporating Christian and Muslim influences) and dynamic (influencing the way each of those religions is practiced in Africa). In fact, one of the interesting features of the way these two major faiths are practiced in Africa is the syncretistic incorporation of African traditional beliefs and practices into both Christian and Islamic worship. It is not unusual for African Christians or Muslims to continue to engage in rituals or practices based on African traditions. For example, a man may attend weekly services at a mosque or church, but still seek out the help of a specialized healer called a witch doctor to protect his family from black magic.

It would be nearly impossible for any book to examine all of the rich details and complexities of religious practice on a continent the size of Africa. This book is intended as an introduction to the history and customs of the traditional religions, Christianity, and Islam as they are practiced in Africa. The second chapter provides a general overview of the beliefs of the African Traditional Religion, attempting to explain the African worldview, and how various types of religious leaders work with the spirit world to protect and help their communities. The third chapter gives an overview of Christianity's history in Africa, from its origins through the mid-20th century. This is followed by a chapter that examines the phenomenon of African Christianity—the Pentecostal form of the religion that has become widespread over the past four decades—as well as the success of mainstream Christianity on the continent. Chapter 5 provides a history about the spread of Islam into Africa between the 7th and 20th centuries, along with discussion of the syncretistic practice of Islam on the continent. Chapter 6 explains the political influence of Islam in Africa after colonialism. The final chapter examines the role of religion in past and current African conflicts, such as the wars in Algeria, Nigeria, Sudan, and Somalia; this chapter also looks at how Islamic law, or Sharia, has been implemented in parts of Africa, often with violent consequences.

2 AFRICAN TRADITIONAL RELIGION

Scholars use the term *African Traditional Religion*, or *ATR*, to describe the many different systems of belief held by indigenous people of the continent. There are about 3,000 ethnic groups in Africa, and each has its own religious system: within any given community, members tell traditional stories, perform certain rituals, and consult religious leaders unique to their ethnic group. However, while two neighboring tribes may tell different stories or perform rituals differently, their traditional religions have many similarities. They share a belief in the existence of a supreme creator and of spirits, and they incorporate many ritual prayers and actions in their everyday life.

For Africans, a person's religion is part of all aspects of his or her world. "[Religious belief] is integrated so much into different areas of life that in fact most of the African languages do not have a word for religion as such," writes the Kenyan theologian John Mbiti. In addition, he notes, individuals form their community

(Opposite) Members of the Nharo San tribe, from the central Kalahari Desert in Botswana, perform a ritual dance to cleanse their minds and bodies of evil spirits.

18

through the practice of their religion: "To be human is to belong to the whole community, and to do so involves participating in the beliefs, ceremonies, rituals, and festivals of that community," Mbiti says. "A person cannot detach himself from the religion of his group, for to do so is to be severed from his roots, his foundation, his context of security, his kinships and the entire group of those who make him aware of his own existence."

African communities do not just include living family and neighbors, but also the Supreme Being, a variety of spirits and lesser gods, and deceased relatives. The interaction of all of these entities forms the basis of religious belief and activity.

A SUPREME BEING

In the African Traditional Religion, a fundamentally good and merciful Supreme Being is believed to have created the universe. In this respect, the faith is monotheistic: people believe in the existence of a single, omnipotent creator god. Some ethnic groups, like the Fon of Benin, see the entity as having both male and female aspects. The Bambara tribe of Mali believes that the Supreme Being consists of four parts, in which the main creator god, called Bemba, coexists with three other gods named Nyale, Faro, and Ndomadyiri. In most tribes, the creator god appears as a father, although a few matriarchal cultures see the Supreme Being as the Great Mother. However, these are human characterizations: all traditional religions agree that the Supreme Being is essentially unknowable.

This creator god sustains life for humans, who are regarded in the African Traditional Religion as the center of the universe. The Supreme Being created the elements that the African people need in order to live well: good weather, crops, and fertility. Subsequently all aspects of the world are viewed in terms of their usefulness to humans: Animals are defined according to whether or not they can be eaten. Plants are valued in terms of whether they can be used as food, as medicine, or for making houses.

According to traditional beliefs, the Supreme Being established universal laws that maintain order, and people can flourish only when they obey these laws. As a result, to maintain the proper relationship with the creator, humans must understand and separate right practices from wrong. When people violate these universal laws and disrupt that relationship, suffering results.

THE SPIRIT WORLD

Although the creator god sustains the universe, in most African cultures he is not believed to participate directly in the world's affairs. Instead, spirits act as intermediaries. This belief in spirits existing separately from physical bodies is called animism. (Followers of the African Traditional Religion are sometimes referred to as animists, although such terminology does not recognize their belief in a supreme power.) There are two kinds of spirits—those found in nature and those of deceased ancestors.

AFRICAN CREATION MYTHS

To Westerners who grew up in the Jewish, Christian, or Muslim faiths, many African creation myths may sound familiar. Usually, humans are said to have lived in paradise or heaven with the Supreme Being. In creation myths originating in Nigeria, Sudan, Kenya, Uganda, and Zambia, the Supreme Being made four people, rather than two. In some cases humans were fashioned from clay. In others, they originated in swamps and crawled out onto the land. Some myths say that the first humans grew on the tree of life as its fruit.

However humans came to be made, most creation stories generally agree that the Supreme Being treated the first people like his children. He taught them how to live and have children of their own. Many African traditional stories recount how the Supreme Being provided the first humans with the tools that they would need to build a society.

At some point, however, humans were separated from the Supreme Being and subsequently afflicted by disease, aging, and death. Some stories state that paradise was lost by accident; for example, some tales say that a cord connected the Supreme Being in heaven with humans on Earth until a hyena ate it. Other myths declare that the Creator was driven off by the annoying sound of a woman threshing grain very loudly.

In many of the myths, women are responsible for the separation of the Supreme Beings and humans. The Bambuti Pygmy tribe, of the Congo region, has a "forbidden fruit" story that is similar to the biblical story of Adam and Eve. In this tale, there is a tree that humans are not supposed to pick from. However, a pregnant woman who craved the fruit convinced her husband to pick it, and upon eating the fruit, brought death to humans.

In some of the stories that blame women for the break between the Supreme Being and humans, the women are named, and often serve as the central figure of the tale. In this way women, who are themselves bearers of new life, are recognized as responsible for both death and life.

Nature spirits inhabit particular places, like mountains and rivers, and may also exist within wild animals. Their power varies according to the beliefs of the tribe. Some African ethnic groups believe nature spirits are so powerful they can control the movement of heavenly bodies, while other groups believe that these spirits affect, but do not control, the sun, moon, and stars. Some

THE NAMES OF GOD

Country	African names for God
Angola	Kalunga, Nzambi, Suku
Botswana	Modimo, Urezhwa
Burundi	Imana
Cameroon	Njinyi, Nyooiy
Dem.Rep. of the Congo	Akongo, Arebati, Djakomba, Katshonde, Kmvoum, Leza, Nzambi
Ethiopia	Arumgimis, Igziabher, Magano, Tel, Tsuossa, Waqa, Yere, Yere, Siezi
Ghana	Bore-Bore, Dzemawon, Mawu, Na'angmin, Nyame, Onyankopon
Ivory Coast	Nyame, Onyankopon
Kenya	Akuj, Asis, Mulungu, Mungu, Ngai, Nyasaye, Tororut, Wele(Were)
Lesotho	Molimo (Modimo)
Liberia	Yala
Madagascar	Andriamanitra, Zanahary
Malawi	Cauta, Chiuta, Leza, Mulungu, Unkurukuru, Utixo
Mozambique	Mulungu
Namibia	Kalunga, Mukuru, Ndjambi Karunga, Pamba
Nigeria	Ondo, Chuku, Hinegba, Olodumare, Olorun, Osanobua, Osowo, Owo, Soko
Rwanda	Imana
Sierra Leone	Leve, Meketa, Ngewo, Yatta
South Africa	Inkosi, Khuzwane, Modimo, Mwari, Raluvhimba, Unkulunkulu, Utixo
Sudan	Ajok, Bel, Dyong, Elo, Jok (Juok, Juong), Kalo, Kwoth, Mbori (Mboli), Nhialic, Nguleso, Ngun Tamukujen
Swaziland	Mkulumncandi, Umkhulumncandi
Tanzania	Enkai, Ishwanga, Kyala, Kyumbi, Mulungu (Murungu), Mungo, Ruwa
Uganda	Akuj, Jok (Juok), Katonda, Kibumba, Ori, Rugaba, Ruhanga, Weri
Zambia	Chilenga, Chiuta, Lesa (Leza), Mulungu, Nyambe, Nzambi, Tilo
Zimbabwe	Unkulunkulu, Mwali (Mwari), Nyadenga

tribes ask the nature spirits for their help, while others simply regard spirits as a way to explain phenomena of the natural world.

Although considered to be less powerful, the human spirits of recently dead ancestors can act on behalf of the living by approaching the Supreme Being to ask for assistance with family members' problems. Generally, Africans invoke the help of ancestors from the past five generations; when no one remembers the name of an ancestor any longer, that person's spirit departs the earthly community.

In many African religions, people believe that individuals are made up of various elements, including moral, social, spiritual, and physical components. If any aspect of the person is out of balance—as a result of moral or spiritual transgressions against the Supreme Being's universal laws—the whole person suffers. A living person's moral or spiritual misdeeds can also damage his or her relationships with family ancestors and with the nature spirits.

Suffering can be individual or community-wide; followers of traditional African religions attribute both a personal illness and a nationwide drought to some kind of spiritual crisis. To end the suffering, it is necessary to repair the spiritual relationship, usually through the guidance of religious leaders, as well as with prayers and offerings.

RELIGIOUS LEADERS

In the African Traditional Religion, people believe there is a mystical power in the universe that is granted by the Supreme Being and accessed by spirits. Some humans can also tap into this magical power, effectively bridging the spiritual world and the physical one. This ability gives them powers to heal others, affect weather, and see the future. These spiritual leaders are believed to carry a special knowledge that gives order to the community and preserves the divine hierarchy. According to

A witch doctor dances during a ceremony in Ghana. The white clay on his face, as well as the white robes he is wearing, symbolizes the purification required to communicate with the spirit world.

traditional beliefs, priests, medicine men and women (healers), mediums, diviners, and rainmakers have the ability to express magic through incantations, charms, prayers, and gestures.

In many African cultures, priests care for the temple or shrine of a specific lesser god. Priests may be either men or women, and in many tribes they gain their positions through training. (There are a few tribes, such as the Baamba, Bavenda, and Sonjo, in which the priesthood is inherited.)

Followers of traditional religions turn to the village medicine man, or traditional doctor, in times of illness, which typically is thought to result from damage to their spiritual relationship with the Supreme Being or lesser deities. Healers offer relief from physical ailments through medicines found in herbs, leaves, roots, fruits, tree barks, insects, eggs, animal parts, and other objects found in nature. Traditional doctors also act as spiritual and social healers, by listening to people's problems and offering advice. Modern doctors working in Africa have long acknowledged that traditional healers can help patients recover psychologically from illnesses.

A person who is suffering from an illness may call on a medium in order to ask the spirits what he or she did to bring on the sickness. Specially trained mediums, who are almost always women, intentionally allow themselves to be possessed by spirits during special dancing and drumming rituals. By allowing spirits to inhabit their bodies, mediums enable spirits to speak directly to others and tell them things they need to know. Through a medium, spirits may also communicate warnings and desires to the community. This knowledge directs the actions of the community as it attempts to appease the spirit world.

Some spiritual leaders are thought to be able to divine, or foresee, the future. Followers of traditional religions believe that diviners can understand the past and present, and predict future events by interpreting messages found in nature, such as randomly scattered pebbles, shells, or animal entrails. Diviners also try to uncover the source of spiritual disturbances believed to be the source of illnesses or personal troubles.

Many African communities also depend on a rainmaker, who is believed to have the ability to influence the weather through a relationship with deities in charge of the rain. It is the job of the rainmaker to ensure that the rains come when needed and stop before crops are ruined by flood. This is accomplished through prayers and rituals performed at certain times of the year.

WITCHCRAFT AND SORCERY

The magic of the African Traditional Religion is neither good nor evil, and can therefore be used for either purpose. While priests,

This West African diviner makes predictions or interprets events by reading grids and symbols in the sand.

healers, mediums, diviners, and rainmakers use magic to help members of their community, witches and sorcerers tap in to spiritual energy to hurt their community, by using black magic.

Some Africans believe that sorcerers and witches have the ability to damage a person's health, family, crops, or livestock. An individual with the knowledge of witchcraft can gain power over another person by obtaining an item belonging to that person and casting spells on it.

When a community suspects that witchcraft is the source of its problems, its members will turn to a specialized healer or diviner called a witch doctor. For example, after a death, family members may consult a diviner to determine whether a witch or sorcerer was responsible for the loss. While Africans understand that everyone must die, they believe that black magic can cause physical ailments, even those associated with old age. People thought to be practicing witchcraft are often killed or expelled from the community.

Many Africans carry charms to protect them against black magic. This belief that an object has magical powers that can help its owner is called fetishism.

PRAYER, OFFERINGS, AND SACRIFICES

In the African Traditional Religion, worshipers believe that prayer and sacrifice allow individuals to communicate with the spiritual world and Supreme Being. Daily prayers commonly express gratitude or requests for good health and protection for their families, crops, and cattle. Prayers may be said before beginning a journey, while preparing to hunt, or in times of illness or trouble.

Individuals and families also communicate with the spiritual world by making offerings and animal sacrifices to the Supreme Being and to the lesser spirits and ancestors. Offerings can consist of foods (such as fruits, maize, nuts, vegetables, honey, or eggs), beverages (such as milk, wine, or water), or objects (such as cloth, money, incense, or ornaments). Sacrifices involve the killing of animals, such as chickens or dogs, which are then presented to the Supreme Being or lesser spirits. Entire com-

Many Africans believe that talismans and amulets, such as the ones this Chadian man is wearing around his neck, have the power to protect the possessor from trouble. These charms vary from area to area, but often are carved with sacred images or enchanted with spells so they ward off evil spirits.

munities typically sacrifice larger animals (such as cattle and sheep) or wild animals.

RITES AND RITUALS

Because African life is chiefly concerned with continuity of the community, large families are desired. Young couples often practice fertility rituals, in which they ask lesser gods or ancestors for help with conceiving a child. Motherhood is considered a sacred calling—a woman's most important contribution to her community and to the universal social order.

Once a woman is pregnant, she must follow specific rules, which vary depending on her culture. In order to ensure a safe and happy birth, she must abide by her tribe's restrictions regarding the eating of certain foods or performing particular activities. For example, a taboo of one ethnic group might forbid her from eating meat that has been killed with poison. Other restrictions might require the pregnant woman to stop sleeping with her husband, or to return to her parents' house and live there until the child is born. During pregnancy, the woman may wear protective charms that are supposed to keep both her and the child safe. After the child is born, the new baby receives a name in a special ceremony.

One of the most important rituals in the life of a child is his or her initiation into adulthood, a ceremony necessary for a person to marry and have children. In many African cultures, this rite of passage involves circumcision rituals for both boys and girls. (In the Western world, the female circumcision ceremony, which involves cutting off part of the girls' clitoris, is considered a barbaric practice, and Africans have been pressured to end the practice.) The blood shed during circumcision rites is said to connect the person to the adult community. Coming of age ceremonies, which typically involve the entire community, often include instruction on how to raise a family and be a responsible member of the village. After they have completed initiation rites, young people are expected to marry and start a family.

Marriage ceremonies vary greatly according to ethnic group. In some places, a groom and his clan may make a mock attack on the bride's home to make it seem like they are stealing her. Sometimes the groom simply comes to her family's house to pick her up. Regardless of the ceremony, marriage celebrations usually include feasting that involves the whole community so everyone can recognize the creation of a new couple. However, the marriage will not be considered complete until it results in the birth of a child.

In most traditional African religions, marriage to more than one wife, or polygamy, is an acceptable practice. Polygamous families can be found in all parts of Africa, although they are less common in some societies. The practice of having multiple wives helps ensure that a family will have a large number of children to help with farming chores, as well as ensure that the spirits of deceased ancestors will continue to receive offerings from the living in the years to come.

In addition to familial ceremonies, various agricultural rites and rituals are also a part of many African cultures. Ceremonies are typically held to ensure the fertility of the soil at planting time and to call forth rain in times of drought. At the end of the growing season, many tribes hold a "first fruits" ritual, in which the harvest is blessed and purified.

A young Masai man, holding two spears, poses in front of a herd of cattle. The mask he is wearing indicates that he has recently gone through a traditional coming-of-age ceremony.

CONTINUING TRADITIONS

There is no written scripture in the African Traditional Religion. Instead traditional practices are reinforced and passed along to younger generations orally, in the form of proverbs, songs, prayers, stories, and religious rituals.

In many African tribes, the drum is an integral part of these ceremonies and rituals. Drumming is essential to dance rituals that lead to trance-possession, explains Jon Michael Spencer, in an article in *The Journal of Religious Thought*. "It was actually rhythm that was responsible," he states, "for the percussiveness produced the power which moved the African to dance and into trance-possession. . . . The supernatural quality of the drum's powerful percussiveness produced the fervent rhythmic monotony prerequisite to the prompting of spirit-possession."

Some African dialects are tonal languages, in which the rising or falling pitch of a word changes its meaning. In West Africa, certain kinds of drums, called "talking drums," allow the drummer to produce varying pitches. By using varying rhythms and tones, the drummer can reproduce the sounds of tonal languages. In the past, talking drums allowed different tribes in West Africa to communicate among themselves. But they also played an important part in traditional African religious ceremonies, often used to tell stories of famous heroes and moral fables. In the Akan culture, in Ghana, the word for drum, *tchreman*, actually means "to educate a nation."

It is estimated that nearly 108 million Africans still practice a tribal or indigenous religion. This figure does not include those who have nominally converted to Christianity or Islam but continue to practice traditional rituals as part of their daily lives.

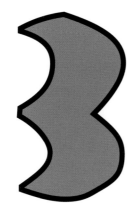

THE SPREAD OF CHRISTIANITY IN AFRICA

hristianity arrived in Africa a few years after the death and resurrection of its primary figure, Jesus Christ. According to the Bible, a man from the upper Nile region may have been one of the first Africans to hear the Christian message of salvation. In the eighth chapter of Acts of the Apostles, Jesus's disciple Philip meets a man described as an Ethiopian. Philip teaches the Ethiopian about Jesus and baptizes him in a nearby stream, after which the man "went on his way rejoicing." Many Christians today believe this man may have been the first African Christian.

During his lifetime Jesus encountered a few Africans. In fact, in the Gospel of Mark a man named Simon from the city of Cyrene in North Africa (modern-day Libya) helped Jesus carry the cross on the way to his crucifixion. The crucifixion—a brutal death demanded by Jewish authorities and carried out by Roman soldiers— is the central event of Christianity, a religion that developed some 2,000 years ago.

THE LIFE OF JESUS

At that time, the entire Mediterranean world (including North Africa and the lands of the Middle East) was under the control of the Roman Empire. Among the subject peoples in the empire were the Jews, who lived in a strip of territory along the eastern Mediterranean that roughly corresponds to the modern state of Israel. The Jews had once been a powerful independent kingdom, but for nearly 500 years they had been ruled by foreign powers—Babylonians, Persians, Greeks, and, beginning around 63 B.C., the Romans. During this period, the Jews came to believe that one day a great leader would free them from oppression and establish a great independent kingdom. This fabled priest-king would be the *moshiach*, or messiah—the savior of the Jews.

Some Jews believed that a man named Jesus, who spent three years preaching in the Galilee region to the north of Jerusalem, was the promised messiah. Jesus was a Jew who had grown up in the small town of Nazareth. When he was about 30 years old he

This Roman fresco depicts the body of Jesus being taken down from the cross after his death. Christianity spread into Roman-ruled North Africa within a few decades of Jesus's death in the first century A.D.

began to teach. Jesus emphasized the importance of obeying the laws recorded in the Jewish scriptures, but also encouraged his followers to focus on spiritual matters and the glorification of God.

Jesus soon gathered a small group of committed followers, who were attracted by his teachings and by the miracles and healings he performed. From this group he selected 12 as his apostles, and he spent three years teaching them. The apostles came to believe Jesus was the messiah, who had come to free them from Roman rule. Instead, Jesus explained, he was the Son of God and had come to save mankind from its sins.

Jewish leaders disagreed with Jesus's teachings, and were offended that he claimed to be the Son of God. When Jesus and the apostles visited Jerusalem for the annual Passover celebration, members of the Sanhedrin collaborated with Roman authorities to have Jesus arrested as a threat to Rome. Jesus submitted to arrest without resisting, and he was humiliated, tortured, and suffered an excruciating death by being nailed to a cross. (The exact date is uncertain, but this event is believed to have occurred around A.D. 29.)

Christians believe that three days after the crucifixion, Jesus rose from the grave. He then continued to teach his followers for 40 days, before ascending into Heaven. Followers of Christianity believe that Jesus died on the cross in order to allow people to enter heaven and be with God after their own deaths.

ORIGINS OF CHRISTIANITY IN AFRICA

The life and ministry of Jesus was detailed in four books, known as the Gospels, which were written several decades after his death and resurrection. The stories of Jesus's early followers are told in the biblical book Acts of the Apostles, as well as in the letters written by such early Christian leaders as Peter, Paul, and John. According to Acts, the apostles began to speak to others about

Jesus Christ. This angered the Jewish religious leaders who had wanted Jesus to be executed, and they began attacking the early Christians. The Christians fled to escape this persecution; this resulted in their taking their new religion to many new lands. Within a relatively short time, Christianity had spread throughout the Roman Empire, which at the time included North Africa.

According to tradition, St. Mark, the author of one of the Gospels, was the first apostle to visit Egypt. Mark is believed to have established a church in the Egyptian city of Alexandria, which was an important center of learning and culture in the ancient world. He was apparently martyred in A.D. 68, during a time when Christians throughout the Roman Empire were being persecuted.

Although it is uncertain exactly when Christianity arrived in Egypt, it is clear that the church flourished there. The Egyptian church that Mark founded became known as the Coptic Church, and Christian writings dating to the middle of the second century A.D. have been found throughout the country.

Alexandria was home to an important catechetical school, where people could be instructed in the principles of Christianity. It had been founded around A.D. 190 by a scholar named Pantanaeus. He was eventually succeeded by his pupil Clement, who became a great theologian and helped to define Christian doctrine. Origen, another pupil of the Alexandrian catechetical school, was among the first major philosophers of the early Christian Church; in his writings, he attempted to explain the nature of God and the divine Trinity of Christian belief (God the Father, Jesus the Son, and the Holy Spirit).

During the first five centuries of the Christian era, North Africa was home to many great Christian thinkers and theologians. Among them was Tertullian, a second-century convert to Christianity who lived in the city of Carthage (in present-day Tunisia). Tertullian lived during a time when Roman authorities persecuted Christians, and he wrote moving essays defending Christian beliefs. In his essay "Apologeticus," he also wrote about the rapid spread of the faith: "We are but of yesterday, and we have filled every place among you—cities, islands, fortresses, towns, market-places, the very camp, tribes, companies, palace, senate, [and] forum."

Another famous theologian of the early church was Athanasius, who played an important role at the Council of Nicaea in 325. At the council, which was called by the Roman emperor Constantine the Great, Christian leaders established the basic principles of the orthodox Christian faith. At the council

GNOSTICISM IN ANCIENT AFRICA

Gnosticism, a movement within early Christianity, flourished in Africa. The Gnostics believed in mysticism, and stressed the importance of knowledge as the way to achieve a closer relationship with God. (By contrast, orthodox Christians taught that there was nothing men could know or do that would bring them closer to God—the relationship was only possible because of the death and resurrection of Jesus Christ.) Gnosticism was greatly influenced by Asian "mystery religions," such as Zoroastrianism from Persia. "Alexandria was probably the world's leading Gnostic centre in the second century A.D.," writes Elizabeth Isichei in *A History of Christianity in Africa*. "Although, ultimately, Gnosticism was condemned as a heresy, many Gnostics lived, taught, and died peacefully within the Catholic Church."

Before the mid-20th century, all that was known about the Gnostics was that they were heretics who had been driven out of the church. Most Gnostic writings were destroyed during the fourth and fifth centuries. But in 1945 an Egyptian farmer discovered a cache of ancient manuscripts buried at a place called Nag Hammadi. When examined by scholars, these texts turned out to be a series of Gnostic books that had been translated from Greek into Coptic, and hidden for nearly 1,600 years. The Gnostic Gospels, as the Nag Hammadi texts came to be known, shed new insights into the beliefs of the Gnostics, as well as the formation of the early Christian Church.

Early Christianity in Africa was very diverse, and distinctive churches have survived in both Egypt and Ethiopia. (Top) A Coptic monastery near Cairo, Egypt. The Coptic Church is the largest Christian group in Egypt today, making up some 9 percent of the population. (Left) An Ethiopian priest in full regalia in Lalibela. The Ethiopian Orthodox Church was the only Christian denomination in sub-Saharan Africa before the colonial era.

Athanasius spoke against the teachings of Arius, another brilliant North African bishop, who held beliefs that most Christians considered heresy.

Perhaps the greatest of the African Christians during the Roman era was St. Augustine of Hippo (354–430). Augustine was a philosopher who wrote many books, including *Confessions* and *The City of God*. He remains one of the most influential Christian theologians.

THE SPREAD OF CHRISTIANITY CHECKED

During the third and fourth centuries, orthodox Christianity spread throughout North Africa. Over time many variations of the religion developed, which church leaders considered to be unorthodox. North Africans identified themselves by their beliefs: Arians, Donatists, Copts, Nestorians, or as members of numerous other sects. Augustine and other writers argued the merits of their particular beliefs through letters, sermons, and essays that were distributed throughout the Roman Empire.

By the end of the fourth century, Christianity was the dominant faith of people living along the Mediterranean coast of Africa. Coptic Christian missionaries even spread their teachings southeast from Egypt to the kingdom of Aksum, in present-day Ethiopia. But there was a natural barrier preventing the spread of Roman religion and ideas to the southern part of the continent—the vast Sahara Desert.

Roman rule in North Africa ended during the fifth century, when an invading tribe from the fringes of the empire, the Vandals, gained control of the province. The Vandals were Arians, who followed the teachings of the controversial Bishop Arius, and they persecuted Roman Catholics in the region.

Rome itself fell to other barbarians around the year 476. However, the Eastern half of the empire persisted, with its capital at Constantinople. The Eastern Roman (or Byzantine) Empire would remain a powerful force in the Mediterranean world, reconquering much of North Africa under the Emperor Justinian in 533. Christian missionaries from Constantinople eventually traveled up the Nile River to the area of modern-day Sudan, where they converted three African kingdoms to Christianity: Nobatia, Makouria, and Alwa.

Many of the early Church's greatest thinkers and writers were from North Africa. Perhaps most important was St. Augustine of Hippo (354–430).

The arrival of another invading force during the seventh century would turn back the spread of Christianity in Africa. Islam was a new religion that emerged from the Arabian Peninsula between 622 and 632. It was based on the teachings of a prophet named Muhammad, who united the Arab tribes under his rule. In 639, seven years after Muhammad's death, the Arab Muslims emerged from the Arabian desert and invaded Egypt, conquering that Byzantine province in 642. The Muslims continued to spread their influence, and by 705 all of North Africa was under their control.

Christians living in Africa under Muslim rule were permitted to practice their faith, so long as they paid extra taxes to the Islamic rulers. Africans who converted to Islam did not have to pay the tax, and they received other benefits and privileges in the new state as well. The Muslims encouraged conquered peoples to convert, and many did. In addition, as Arabs settled in the newly conquered territories, they married Christian women and their children were raised as Muslims. Over a period of several centuries, Christianity was gradually replaced by Islam as the dominant faith of North Africa. This change was largely complete by the 11th century. The only significant Christian communities that survived were the Copts in Egypt (a minority under Muslim rule) and the Christians of Aksum, in modern-day Ethiopia, which was surrounded by Muslim states.

THE RETURN OF CHRISTIANITY

During the 15th century, European countries emerged from centuries of isolation and began exploring the world's oceans. The primary reason for the so-called Age of Exploration (1420–1620) was the search for economic resources. The rulers of countries like Portugal, Spain, Holland, Great Britain, and France sent out expeditions looking for trade routes that would enrich their kingdoms.

THE LEGEND OF PRESTER JOHN

For centuries, Muslims and Christians fought for control over lands in North Africa, Europe, the Middle East, and Central Asia. During the eighth century, Muslim armies from North Africa invaded and conquered the Iberian Peninsula (the location of modern-day Spain and Portugal). The European Christians fought back, and over several hundred years they succeeded in forcing the Muslims out of Western Europe.

In Europe, while these wars were going on, a legend developed during the 12th century about a Christian kingdom ruled by a wise man named Prester John. The kingdom was believed to be somewhere in Africa, beyond the Muslim lands. Many Christians—including Prince Henry the Navigator of Portugal—hoped that they could one day collaborate with Prester John's kingdom to outflank and destroy their Muslim enemies. In fact, one of the goals of Prince Henry's Portuguese voyages of exploration during the 15th century was to make contact with Prester John.

Belief in Prester John was so widespread that his figure often appeared on maps of the time. However, by the end of the Age of Exploration it was obvious that his Christian kingdom in Africa was nothing more than a myth.

Portugal led the way: beginning in 1420, a member of the Portuguese ruling family, Prince Henry the Navigator, sent a series of expeditions south to explore the coast of Africa. Their purpose was to find a sea route to Asia, so that Portuguese merchants could bypass the long and dangerous land route through Muslim-held lands on the continent. As the Portuguese worked their way south, they established trading posts at the places where they stopped. These were sites where later expeditions could stop for water and food, as well as trade with African tribes living nearby. The Portuguese traded iron and European goods for gold, ivory, and slaves.

The main purpose of these voyages was economic, but the Portuguese also preached their Roman Catholic faith to the Africans. During the early 16th century Jesuit missionaries succeeded in converting the rulers of the powerful African kingdom of Kongo to Christianity. The church planted by the Jesuits was later nourished by Capuchin monks from Italy, and it was still in existence when other Christian missionaries arrived in the region during the 19th century. Other churches were established on São Thomé Island, the Cape Verde Islands,

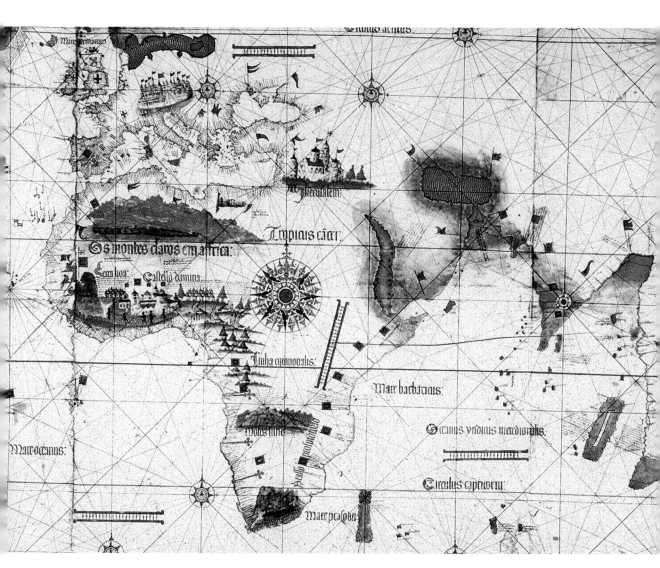

This Portuguese map from 1501 shows the discoveries of Vasco da Gama and other seafarers during the 15th century. The Portuguese had charted the west coast of Africa for more than 80 years, so it is more detailed on the map; however, the coastlines of East Africa and India, which had not been reached until Gama's 1497–99 voyage, are inaccurate. Portuguese trading posts on the African coast are marked with crosses and flags; small figures represent the areas in West Africa where captured Africans were sold as slaves.

and in parts of West Africa, including the Gold Coast and the Niger Delta region.

Although these Christian churches survived, over the years Christian teachings were usually combined with traditional African religious traditions and beliefs. Later missionaries found this syncretistic form of Christianity when they arrived in Africa.

Portugal's control over the African coast, and its discovery of a route around the continent to Asia, made it the wealthiest country in Europe for a time. However, Portugal was too small to maintain a vast overseas empire, and other European countries soon encroached on its holdings. It was from these countries that new missionaries would begin coming to Africa during the 19th century. But unlike the Portuguese, who attempted to spread the Roman Catholic faith, missionaries from Britain, Germany, Holland, and other countries were bringing a newer variation of the Christian faith, known as Protestantism.

For centuries Roman Catholicism had been the dominant form of Christianity in Europe, but during the 15th and 16th centuries a reform movement gained strength. Led by men like Martin Luther, John Calvin, and John Knox, new Christian churches were established outside the control of the Catholic pope. Referred to as Protestant churches, they included Lutheran, Presbyterian, Baptist, Anglican, and many other denominations.

WORK OF THE MISSIONARIES

By the early 18th century, Protestant church organizations like the Anglican Church's Society for the Propagation of the Gospel in Foreign Parts were sending missionaries to convert the indigenous peoples of North America. Eventually, such societies began to send missionaries to Africa as well. Missionaries were inspired by the "Great Commission," a statement of Jesus that was recorded at the end of the Gospel of Matthew: "All authority in heaven

CHRISTIANITY AND THE ATLANTIC SLAVE TRADE

For most of the Europeans who visited Africa during the 15th, 16th, and 17th centuries, spreading the Gospel to Africans was a secondary concern. Their primary purpose was to purchase slaves and transport them across the Atlantic to settlements in the New World. Slave labor was needed to work Spanish and Portuguese mines and farms in South America and the Caribbean, and later to serve English colonists in North America.

The idea of Christians buying and selling slaves contradicts the so-called Golden Rule; in the Gospel of Luke, Jesus instructed his disciples, "Do to others as you would have them do to you." (Luke 6: 31). However, Christians of the day were apparently not troubled by this contradiction. For example, John Newton, author of the famous hymn "Amazing Grace," was an English slave trader. Even after Newton became a Christian in 1748, he continued to make slaving voyages to Africa. "I never knew sweeter or more frequent hours of divine communion than in my last two voyages to Guinea [to pick up a cargo of slaves]," he later wrote. (Newton did eventually decide that the slave trade was wrong, and gave up his involvement.)

It should be noted that, although Christians participated in the African slave trade, Christian abolitionists also had an important role in ending slavery. During the late 18th century, groups like the Quakers, as well as evangelical Protestants, pressured the governments of Great Britain and the United States to halt the slave trade. In 1807, the British government banned the transatlantic slave trade, and the United States halted the importation of new slaves. France ended slavery in 1815, and countries like Spain and Portugal gave up transporting slaves to their colonies during the 1820s. Today, experts estimate that over 400 years, beginning in 1441, approximately 10 million Africans were taken from Africa as slaves.

and on earth has been given to me. Therefore, go and make disciples of all nations, baptizing them in the name of the Father and of the Son and of the Holy Spirit, and teaching them to obey everything I have commanded you" (Matthew 28: 18–20).

Among the first Protestant missionaries were freed African slaves from America, who had supported the British during the American Revolution and fled to Canada after 1787, once that war was lost. These former slaves, who had converted to Christianity, were eventually transported to West Africa, where they helped establish the British colony that would become Sierra Leone.

Early in the 19th century, white European and American missionaries began to set up mission stations and villages throughout sub-Saharan Africa. For the most part, these missionaries were deeply committed Christians, determined to save the Africans through conversion. The missionaries often tried to integrate themselves into the local culture as they worked to spread the Gospel. Many of the missionaries were great letter writers, so modern historians and students know a great deal about their views of the African people during this period. Unfortunately, less is known about the perspective of the indigenous tribes toward Christianity.

Perhaps the most famous Christian missionary of the 19th century was David Livingstone (1813–1873), who was one of the first Europeans to explore the interior of Africa. Between 1852 and 1856, as a member of the London Missionary Society, Livingstone crossed the continent. During his travels, he attempted to spread Christianity in central Africa, and his 1858 book *Missionary Travels and Researches in South Africa* inspired a new generation of missionaries. Livingstone later explored the Zambezi River and searched for the source of the Nile in southeast Africa.

Within the Anglican Church, some Africans achieved powerful positions in

The Scottish doctor and explorer David Livingstone (1813–1873), pictured here holding a map of Africa, was among the most famous Christian missionaries of the 19th century. Livingstone explored much of southeastern Africa, opening the region for other European missionaries.

the clergy. In 1865, Samuel Ajayi Crowther, who had trained and been ordained as a minister in London, became the first African Bishop in the Anglican Church. He had operated a mission in Nigeria and helped translate religious tracts into local indigenous languages, including Yoruba, Igbo, and Nupe. In a few cases, 19th-century black Africans were ordained as archdeacons, a clergy position subordinate to that of bishop in the Anglican Church.

However, in general Africans had little opportunity to hold important positions in the Christian churches planted by missionaries. For example, the Roman Catholic Church did not

Although European colonialism produced lasting negative effects on Africa, there were positive benefits to the work of missionaries as well, including the establishment of schools and medical centers. In this 1948 photograph a class in the Ganta Missionary School in Liberia practices a writing exercise.

appoint an African bishop until the 1930s. For the most part, whites held most Christian leadership positions, even at the local level: black Africans were rarely anointed to serve as priests or ministers. Often, the highest church position a black African could attain was the status of catechist, a layperson permitted to read during the liturgy and teach new Christians the basic tenets of the faith.

CHANGES IN MISSIONARY ROLE

Missionary activity increased between 1880 and 1920, the high point of European colonialism in Africa. It was during this time that European powers carved up the continent into spheres of influence—a process that began in the 1880s, when representatives of 14 European countries met in Berlin, Germany, to formally divide the continent among themselves. In the years that followed, missionaries often worked hand-in-hand with colonial administrators to change the traditional African cultures and spread European social and moral precepts to the people along with religious beliefs.

Missionaries had long stressed the importance of education and literacy. During the 19th century, the Bible had been translated into numerous African languages. The expansion of colonialism led to an increased demand for schools, to educate a new generation of African leaders. Because missionaries often ran these schools, they became breeding grounds for new converts. In fact, the buildings used as schools during the week often served as churches on Sundays.

As a result, conversion to Christianity also meant acceptance of the colonial culture. Africans were encouraged to give up their traditional practices and embrace the religion and culture of the European colonial powers; those who did became the elite members of the colony, placed in positions of power from which they could continue to advance Christianity and colonial policies.

Although many later African scholars have condemned the missionaries' involvement in the colonial system, which enabled the Europeans to dominate and subjugate the Africans, missionaries did have a positive effect on African culture in some respects. For example, they worked to eliminate such brutal practices as torture and human sacrifice, which were common among some indigenous peoples of Africa.

Missionary activities in Africa continued vigorously through 1940, and brought about great change. They provided people on the low rungs of society with opportunities for advancement, by undermining traditional social systems and depriving former leaders of their authority. Missionary schools increased literacy as Africans had improved access to education. However, at the same time, the negative European attitude about traditional African society diminished the pride the people had in their culture.

GROWTH AND CHANGE

Thanks to the work of the missionaries, by the end of the 19th century the Christian Church had grown to about 10 million in sub-Saharan Africa. Although this was less than 10 percent of the total population, with each convert seeds were being planted for the more explosive growth in the church population that would occur during the 20th century.

But despite the gradual growth of Christianity, and the importance of African converts, few Africans were trained to serve as pastors of mission churches, even though there were shortages of European clergy. (One priest would often have to serve 20 or more rural villages.) This situation frustrated many African Christians, and contributed to a period of great change during the 20th century.

4 CHRISTIANITY IN AFRICA TODAY

During the first half of the 20th century, Christianity spread steadily through sub-Saharan Africa. In 1900, there were an estimated 10 million African Christians, or about 8 percent of the continent's total population of about 120 million. By 1950, the number of Christians on the continent had risen to 34 million, or about 17 percent of the population of 198 million.

But although the Christian community was growing, many Africans were dissatisfied with the Christianity of the mission churches planted by Westerners. White Europeans dominated the church hierarchies of the mission churches. More importantly, the way in which Westerners practiced Christianity was not spiritually fulfilling for many Africans. As John Mbiti writes in *African Religions and Philosophy*:

> Mission Christianity has come to mean for many Africans simply a set of rules to be observed, promises to be expected in the next world, rhythmless hymns to be sung, rituals to be followed and a few other outward things. It

is a Christianity which is locked up six days a week, meeting only for two hours on Sunday and perhaps once during the week. It is a Christianity which is active in a church building. The rest of the week is empty. Africans, who traditionally do not know religious vacuum, feel that they don't get enough religion from this type of Christianity, since it does not fill up their whole life and understanding of the universe. Furthermore, African Christians often feel complete foreigners in mission Churches.

Beginning in the early decades of the 20th century, frustrated African Christians began to break away from the established mission churches, forming their own uniquely African churches. The purpose of these new African Independent Churches (AICs) was to change the impression of Christianity as a "white man's religion," and make the religion more meaningful and appealing to Africans.

Considering the history of the Protestant movement, it is not surprising that most of the African Independent Churches emerged from Protestant denominations. Historically, as differences have emerged in Protestant churches, dissenters have found it easier to break off and establish new denominations, instead of trying to compromise on agreeable practices.

An important difference between mission churches and African Independent Churches is that missionaries taught from a Western cultural perspective, while the African churches view and interpret Christian beliefs through the African cultural experience. AICs reject most of the "pagan" rituals and practices of traditional African religions, but three basic elements of traditional thought are retained. One is the concept of a Supreme Being, who is comparable to the Christian God. A second is the belief in evil spirits that cause sickness and misfortune, and third is belief in the power of ritual prayers and acts to keep these spirits at bay.

Like most Protestant denominations, nearly all AICs stress the Bible, rather than clerical pronouncements, as the ultimate authority. Many Africans read the Bible literally, and accept Old Testament practices that Western missionaries might dismiss as superstitious nonsense, but which conformed to traditional African culture. For example, such practices as exorcism of evil spirits, control over the rain, or faith healing—all of which are mentioned in the Bible—appealed to African believers and are accepted practices in most AICs.

"African Christians longed for sources of spiritual power," writes Elizabeth Isichei in *A History of Christianity in Africa*. "They found in the Bible a world of victory over sickness and death, of mastery over evil spirits. . . . The emphasis on healing and miracle was not wholly absent from the mission churches, but, typically, they interpreted disease in a rationalist-scientific way, and relied more on hospitals than prayer to solve health problems."

Many of the AICs are considered Pentecostal denominations. Pentecostals share with other denominations the basic Christian beliefs of the divinity and nature of Jesus and his saving sacrifice

African Christians in Sierra Leone depart from their Pentecostal church after a Sunday worship service. The building's new construction indicates that the church is expanding to meet the needs of its growing congregation.

on the cross. Additionally, though, they believe that those who pray and accept Jesus as Lord will be filled with the Holy Spirit, and this will give them the power to accomplish great miracles, such as healing the sick or driving out evil spirits. Such events were common among the Christians of the first century, as recorded in Acts of the Apostles and other books of the New Testament. Christians who believe that modern-day people can experience and transmit the power of the Holy Spirit to perform miracles are sometimes called charismatics. (This name comes from the Greek word *charis*, which means "grace" and denotes a spiritual power given by the grace of God.)

The development of AICs has led to explosive growth in the Christian population of Africa. In 1970, the Christian population of sub-Saharan Africa was estimated at 117 million. Today, it is estimated at more than 470 million, or over 45 percent of the continent's total population. Many of these African Christians

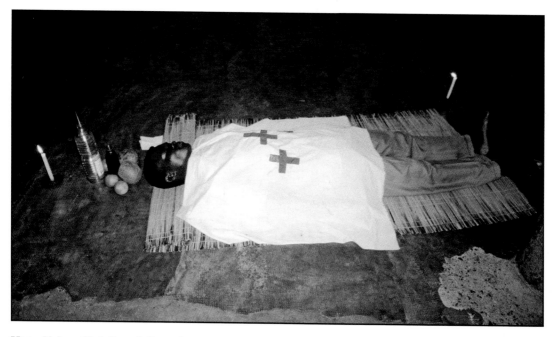

Many African Christians believe that evil spirits cause sickness, and that these spirits can be driven out through the power of prayers and rituals. In this photograph of a Christian healing ceremony in Benin, candles and offerings have been placed at the sick man's head and feet.

are members of one of the more than 7,000 different African Independent Churches. This chapter will briefly examine some of the history and beliefs of three of the largest churches: the Kimbanguist Church in central Africa, the Aladura Churches of western Africa, and the Zion Christian Church of southern Africa.

THE KIMBANGUIST CHURCH

One of the largest African Independent Churches began with the charismatic ministry of a Congolese man named Simon Kimbangu in the early 1920s. Kimbangu was a member of the English Baptist Mission Church in the Belgian Congo, where he taught at a mission school and preached the Gospel to fellow Africans. He established his new church after he claimed to hear a life-changing message: "I am Christ," the voice said. "My servants [the European missionaries] are unfaithful. I have chosen you to witness before your brethren and to convert them. Tend my flock."

Many factors, both local and international, made Africans open to religious conversion at this time. The First World War (1914–18) had dramatically changed the map of the world, as old empires were broken up and new countries created. Millions had died in a worldwide flu pandemic (1918–19). In the Belgian Congo, the colonial authorities had forced many Africans into virtual slave labor on a railroad project. In addition, Africans were ready to accept a form of Christianity that was different from the one preached by the missionaries.

Kimbangu gained a reputation as a healer, and soon people hoping for miracles began visiting his hometown of Nkamba. Declaring himself a prophet, Kimbangu soon had a large following. He taught that people should become Christians, follow biblical teachings, and reject traditional practices involving sorcery and the spirit world. Nkamba became known as the "New Jerusalem."

Kimbangu's success attracted the attention of the Belgian authorities, and the sect was soon banned. After hundreds of Kimbangu's followers were arrested, the prophet himself surrendered voluntarily. In 1921, the colonial authorities sentenced him to death as an enemy of the state, but the sentence was later commuted to life imprisonment, and he was sent to prison in the city of Lubumbashi (then known as Elizabethville).

Although Kimbangu died in prison in 1951, the religious movement he had started lived on after his arrest. His followers often held secret meetings in remote areas, to avoid censure by colonial authorities. In 1959, shortly before the Belgian Congo became an independent country, colonial authorities declared the Kimbanguist Church a legal religion. (Its official name is the Church of Jesus Christ on Earth Through the Prophet Simon Kimbangu.) Most Christian denominations recognize the Kimbanguist Church as Christian, and it has been a member of the World Council of Churches since 1969. Today, its membership is estimated at around 3 million, making it the largest independent church in central Africa.

The head of the church is Joseph Diangienda, the youngest son of Simon Kimbangu. He has shifted the emphasis of the church from its original healing ministry to something closer to the mainstream Christian denominations of the West. Benjamin C. Ray explains in *African Religions: Symbol, Ritual, and Community*:

> The church teaches that there was only one Prophet who performed healing and that was Kimbangu and his original disciples. Now that they have all passed away, healing is accomplished by faith and prayer not by the charismatic power of the Holy Spirit. Nevertheless, the pilgrims to Nkanga carry home water from the sacred spring and the earth from the ground for purposes of healing. In curtailing the charismatic character of early Kimbanguism, Diangienda . . . transformed it into a European missionlike institution. Instead of the charisma of healing, there is now a large and successful organization of schools, medical dispensaries, farming projects, and an educated elite to carry on the growth of the church.

THE ALADURA CHURCHES

At around the same time that the Kimbanguist Church was forming, religious leaders of the Yoruba ethnic group in southwestern Nigeria were establishing their own charismatic churches. The emphasis of these churches, which have spread throughout West Africa, is on the power of prayer. While the churches have various names, all are commonly known as Aladura Churches, from the Yoruba word *aladura*, meaning "those who pray."

The Church of the Lord was founded in 1930, after a Yoruba named Josiah O. Oshitelu began having visions during the mid-1920s in which God called him to spread his teachings. Oshitelu soon began spreading a new message—one that got him dismissed from the Anglican Church: the problems of the world

Evangelical preachers often draw huge crowds in Africa, as is the case with this Christian rally in Lagos, Nigeria.

could be resolved through faith in God, fervent prayer, and frequent fasting.

The Yoruba were experiencing many problems during the 1920s, including an epidemic of bubonic plague and a widespread economic collapse. Anglican missionaries had succeeded in spreading the religion, but many African Christians still kept their traditional rituals. Oshitelu taught that Africans needed to make an absolute commitment to Christianity, and break completely from their pagan past.

"Aladuras retained the belief in the reality of malevolent spirits and witches, and they needed a Christian means to cope with them," writes Benjamin Ray. "The Aladuras emphasized that it was the power of prayer, or *adura*, not pagan divination and sacrifice, that engaged God, together with Jesus Christ and the angels, against the evil forces of this world. Thus the Aladuras molded Christianity into a prophet-led healing system based on the power of Christian prayer, revelation, and ritual practice."

Prayer is at the basis of the Church of the Lord's teachings, and church members have access to a variety of prayer books, rituals, and chants. If the prayer is fervent enough, the Aladuras believe, God will be moved to resolve their personal problems.

Today, the Church of the Lord has some 2 million members, and has spread beyond Nigeria to Ghana, Liberia, Sierra Leone, and other parts of West Africa. The faith has even moved out of Africa, to the United States and Great Britain. The Church of the Lord has been a member of the World Council of Churches since 1975.

There are many other African Independent Churches that are part of the Aladura movement. Other significant Aladura churches include the Celestial Church of Christ, the Precious Stone Society, Christ Apostolic Church, and the Cherubim and Seraphim Society.

THE ZION CHRISTIAN CHURCH

Pentecostalism arrived in southern Africa with a visit by John Graham Lake, a Methodist preacher and businessman from the United States who was a member of a Pentecostal religious community called Zion City, based near Chicago. In April 1908, Lake led a group of missionaries to Johannesburg, South Africa, and began to spread the Pentecostal message. He spent four years in southern Africa, where he founded a large Pentecostal church called the Apostolic Faith Mission.

In the 1910s, a member of the Apostolic Faith Mission, Engenas Lekganyane, broke away and started a new church after receiving what he believed to be a revelation from God. He named the new denomination the Zion Christian Church. Today, it is the largest AIC in southern Africa, with 4 million members, and is currently one of the fastest growing churches in Africa.

Some beliefs and practices of the Zion Christian Church are similar to those of the Presbyterian Church, reflecting the fact that Lekganyane had originally been converted to Christianity by Scottish missionaries. However, the Zionist Christian Church is first and foremost a Pentecostal denomination. Members of the church believe that bishops can perform miracles and healings through the power of the Holy Spirit. They also believe that church leaders (known as *moruti*, or prophets) can communicate with ancestors through the Holy Spirit. The church prohibits its

OTHER NOTABLE PENTACOSTAL CHURCHES

Many other African Independent Churches have contributed to the growth of the Christian faith in Africa. These include the Deeper Life Bible Church in Nigeria, which holds Sunday services attended by more than 100,000 people. Another church that originated in Nigeria, the Redeemed Christian Church of God, now has faith communities all over the world.

members from drinking alcohol, smoking, or eating pork, and condemns sexual promiscuity and violence. The church's Easter celebration is an annual highlight, as more than a million worshippers come to the Zion Christian Church's headquarters at Zion City Moria, in the Limpopo Province of South Africa, for several days of religious services.

After its founder died in 1948, the church split into two denominations. The larger retained the name Zion Christian Church and was led by Lekganyane's oldest son, Edward. The smaller group, led by another son, Joseph, took the name Saint Engenas Zion Christian Church. The churches have spread from South Africa into neighboring countries, including Botswana and Zimbabwe.

MAINSTREAM CHURCHES ALSO GROWING

The rapid growth of the African Independent Churches has attracted a lot of attention. But more common Christian denominations—the so-called mission churches—are also flourishing in Africa. The largest of the mainstream churches is the Roman Catholic Church, which was first brought to sub-Saharan Africa by Portuguese missionaries in the 15th and 16th centuries. Today, according to church statistics, there are an estimated 150 million Catholics in Africa, or about 17 percent of the total population.

The Catholic Church's landmark Second Vatican Council (1962–65) had a great impact on Catholicism in Africa. Among the changes permitted by Vatican II was greater freedom to conduct worship services, including the use of local languages, rather than Latin, and incorporation of different types of music. As a result, the Catholic liturgy in Africa became more appealing to Africans, thanks to the use of traditional music and native language. "It may seem odd, but it is probably true, that the most

Pope Benedict XVI (left), head of the Roman Catholic Church from 2005 to 2013, speaks to an African priest during an ordination mass at the Vatican. In recent decades, the number of Roman Catholic priests from Africa has increased dramatically.

important single effect in Africa in popular terms of the [Vatican] Council has been the change in singing, in hymns, in music, in the use of musical instruments," writes Adrian Hastings in *African Catholicism*. "The pre-Conciliar African Church set its heart on the possession of a harmonium [a type of organ]. The post-Conciliar African Church glories in its use of drums."

Another effect of Vatican II was that black Africans came to dominate church leadership on the continent. Before the council, most priests and virtually all Catholic bishops in Africa were whites from Europe or the United States. After Vatican II, most of these church leaders began to leave Africa as a new generation of African clergy was trained. In 1994, when Pope John Paul II presided over a synod of African bishops, about 90 percent of the church leadership was African.

A distinctive feature of the African Catholic Church is its dependence on catechists—educated laypeople who are in charge of small village churches. The system of catechists developed during the colonial period, as a way to expedite the spread of the Gospel. Catechists teach others the basics of the Christian faith

THE CATHOLIC CHURCH IN AFRICA

The challenge of the Roman Catholic Church in Africa, as outlined in the 1994 synod, is evangelization of the continent. Church leaders are also committed to helping to heal and improve African societies, by working to eliminate the problems created by political corruption, tribal and ethnic conflicts, and widespread poverty.

and lead weekly worship services. In many villages that are too small to have a church staffed by a priest, or in countries where Catholicism is persecuted by the state, catechists help worshippers maintain their faith. But because catechists, unlike priests, are not permitted to administer the sacraments—baptism, communion, confirmation, ordination to the priesthood, penance, marriage, and anointing of the sick (the last rites)—the African Catholic Church has not placed as much emphasis on the sacraments as Catholic Churches in the United States and the West have.

Another of the mainstream churches that is growing is the Anglican Church, which has about 36 million members. According to ChristianityToday.com, the church is growing at an annual rate of 5 percent, making it one of the fastest-growing denominations on the continent. Because of its English roots, the Anglican Church is strongest in countries once ruled as colonies by Great Britain. Nigeria has an Anglican population of about 15 million, while Kenya has 2.5 million Anglicans and South Africa has 2 million. Other Anglican communities can be found in Sudan, Tanzania, Uganda, and in the countries of West Africa and southern Africa.

The Anglican Church has played a particularly important role in South Africa. After the Soweto riots in 1976, Bishop Desmond Tutu and other Anglican clergymen pressured South Africa's government to abolish the apartheid system, a legal method of discrimination against black South Africans. Tutu and other Anglican leaders spoke out against the racist system both at home and abroad, encouraged the United States and other Western nations to impose an economic boycott on South Africa, and helped form the anti-apartheid political party United Democratic Front. After the apartheid system was abolished in 1994, Tutu—who had long spoken about the need for all South African racial groups to reunite and resolve their differences peacefully—was chosen to head the Truth and Reconciliation Committee (a government commission set up to help South Africans deal with the violence and human rights abuses of apartheid).

More recently, the Anglican Church in South Africa has embarked on an ambitious program to help those suffering from HIV/AIDS. In South Africa, the disease has become a devastating epidemic, with nearly 6 million people infected as of 2012, according to UNAIDS. The Anglican Church program attempts to educate Africans about the dangers of unprotected sex and intravenous drug use, both of which can easily spread HIV/AIDS; the Church also provides drugs and treatment programs for South Africans who are already infected.

Anglican leaders in other countries have also worked to bring about change for the better in Africa. In Kenya during the 1980s and 1990s, Bishop David Gitari and other church leaders were threatened and arrested for boldly denouncing the corruption

Archbishop Desmond Tutu, the former head of the Anglican Church in South Africa, is among the continent's best-known religious leaders. Tutu received the Nobel Peace Prize in 1984 for his efforts to end South Africa's apartheid system.

and human rights violations of President Daniel arap Moi. In Uganda during the 1990s, Bishop Gershom Ilukor ignored threats by both government and rebel leaders because of his efforts to end a rebellion in the province where he was the chief Anglican administrator.

Other Protestant churches also continue to flourish in Africa. The Lutheran Church claims 14 million followers on the continent. Many live in the former German colonies of Tanzania and Cameroon, and there are also significant Lutheran communities in Ethiopia, Malawi, and South Africa. There are 7 million Baptists in Africa, making the continent home to that sect's second-largest population (after North America). More than 2 million Baptists live in Nigeria, and nearly 2 million live in the Democratic Republic of the Congo. Communities of Presbyterians and Methodists can also be found in many countries.

NEW LEADERSHIP, AND NEW PROBLEMS

Because of the rapid growth of Christianity in Africa, the continent has gained importance in international religious affairs. This is reflected in the growing number of Africans taking leadership roles. For example, in 2004 Kenyan Samuel Kobia became head of the World Council of Churches, an international ecumenical organization, and Setri Nyomi, an Evangelical Presbyterian from Ghana, has served as chief executive of the World Alliance of Reformed Churches since 2000.

In the United States, the growing importance of African churches can be seen at local levels. For example, the number of Americans ordained to the priesthood by the Roman Catholic Church has declined dramatically since the mid-1960s. As a result, it is becoming more common for priests from Africa—where the number of ordinations more than doubled during the 1990s—to be sent to serve in many Catholic parishes in the United States.

5 THE SPREAD OF ISLAM IN AFRICA

slam is one of the world's major religions, and is practiced by more than 1.6 billion people worldwide. The religion slowly spread throughout Africa over centuries, following long-established trade routes.

THE ORIGINS OF ISLAM

The word *Islam* is derived from the Arabic verb *aslama*, which means "to submit." The founding prophet of Islam, Muhammad (ca. 570–632) taught his followers that they must submit themselves to the will of Allah (or God). Muhammad's followers became known as *Muslims*, or "those who submit."

Muhammad was a member of a poor, but respected, Arab tribe that lived near the city of Mecca, on the Arabian Peninsula. At the time, the Arabs were polytheistic, worshipping a variety of gods and idols; Mecca was an important religious center because it was home to the Kabaa, a shrine in which many of these idols were kept. As a young man, Muhammad worked on trading caravans that traveled between Mecca and the city of Damascus, a large and important center of trade in Syria. These travels exposed Muhammad to various religious systems, including Judaism, Christianity, and Zoroastrianism.

According to stories about Muhammad, he was a good and honest man, and spent time each year alone, praying and reflecting on the injustice and cruelty that were part of Arab society. One night in the year 610, when Muhammad was about 40 years old, he was praying alone in a cave when the angel Gabriel appeared to him. The angel told Muhammad that he had been chosen to tell the world that there was only one God, Allah. Muhammad was frightened and confused, but when he returned home his wife and cousin comforted him. Over the next two years, Muhammad received other revelations from Allah, which he gradually began to share with his family and friends in Mecca.

By 613, Muhammad's private preaching had attracted a group of about 30 committed followers. After Allah told Muhammad to proclaim his message to a wider audience, Muhammad began to speak out in the streets of Mecca, telling the people that they should worship only Allah. Many of the Arabs—particularly the wealthy leaders of Meccan society—resisted this message. Ending the worship of idols, as Muhammad demanded, would have hurt the local economy, because people would stop making pilgrimages to the Kaaba to worship their gods. To stop this dangerous teaching, Meccan leaders passed laws prohibiting all business and social relations with Muhammad and his followers. This began a period of intense persecution for the Muslims of Mecca. Some were killed for their beliefs; Muhammad himself was beaten and threatened with death. As the persecution grew worse, Muhammad even sent a small group of his followers to Africa, where they found shelter in the Christian kingdom of Aksum.

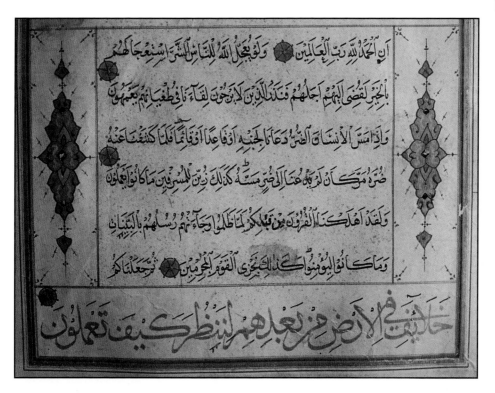

An ornate page from the Qur'an, the holy scripture of Islam. Muslims believe that all of Allah's messages to Muhammad are recorded in the Qur'an, and use the scripture as a guide to proper behavior.

In 622, Muhammad and about 200 of his followers moved north from Mecca to the village of Yathrib. This important event became known as the *hijra*, from an Arabic word meaning "to migrate" or "to leave one's tribe." The tribe was the basis of Arab society, so for Muhammad to leave Mecca was a rejection of Arab tradition. In its place Muhammad developed the idea of a new social framework based on shared religious belief—the *umma*, or Muslim community. Members of the *umma* are expected to protect and defend each other regardless of their previous tribal or family relations. Acceptance of this new social ideal was an important act of faith for Muhammad's followers. In Yathrib (later called Medina, or "city of the Prophet"), Muhammad united the different tribes of the village under his concept of *umma*, and established the first mosque, or place of worship.

CORE ISLAMIC BELIEFS

Islam is more than a religion; it is a way of life. Submission to Allah involves following His regulations concerning everyday life, commerce, and social relations. These regulations are found in the Qur'an, the holy scriptures of Islam. The Qur'an is a collection of the teachings Muhammad received from Allah, which were compiled after the Prophet's death. All committed Muslims observe five important obligations, known as the five pillars of Islam. These include the profession of faith (*shahada*), daily prayer (*salat*), giving charity to those in need (*zakat*), fasting during the month of Ramadan (*sawm*), and the pilgrimage to Mecca (*hajj*).

The profession of faith in God is a prerequisite for anyone who wishes to join the Muslim community. It involves a simple statement: "There is no god but Allah, and Muhammad is His prophet."

Muslims reaffirm this faith during their daily prayers, which are recited at dawn, noon, mid-afternoon, sunset, and evening. When praying, Muslims face in the direction of Mecca. Although Muslims can perform most of the prayers either by themselves or with others, they are required to worship together at noon on Fridays.

The third pillar of Islam is the obligation of Muslims to help the poor, which is stressed throughout the Qur'an. There are two forms of charitable giving: a mandatory tax (*zakat*) and voluntary almsgiving (*sadaqa*).

Between 624 and 630, soldiers from Mecca and Yathrib fought a series of battles. The war ended in January 630, when Muhammad led a large army to Mecca and captured the city without a fight. Muhammad destroyed the idols in the Kaaba, dedicating the sacred shrine to Allah, and the Meccans agreed to follow Muhammad's teachings. By the time Muhammad died two years later, most of the Arabs had become Muslims, and they were ready to spread their new faith beyond the Arabian Peninsula.

ISLAM EXPANDS INTO NORTH AFRICA

After Muhammad's death in 632, the Arabs began to invade neighboring territories. Armies moved east into the Persian

The fourth pillar of Islam is the command to fast during Ramadan, one of the 12 months of the Islamic lunar calendar. Ramadan is considered a sacred month because it was during this month that Muhammad received his first revelations from Allah. During Ramadan, Muslims refrain from eating, drinking, and certain other behaviors from dawn to sunset each day. The purpose of the fast is to practice physical and spiritual discipline, to serve as a reminder of the trials of the poor, and to build a sense of solidarity among all Muslims. At the end of Ramadan, Muslims celebrate with a three-day holiday known as Eid al-Fitr.

The fifth pillar of Islam calls for Muslims to make a pilgrimage to Mecca at least once during their lives, provided they are physically and financially able to do so. Muslims from all walks of life make the journey to Mecca, and the pilgrimage is a powerful spiritual experience.

While the five pillars are prescribed in the Qur'an, the scripture often does not contain specific instructions about religious or social practices. For example, the Qur'an says that Muslims should pray, but does not explain how they should pray. As a result, through centuries of study and discussion Muslims developed a catalog of restrictions and obligations that became known as Sharia. This body of rules, sometimes called Islamic law, is observed by devout Muslims today.

Empire, which was soon conquered by the Muslims. Arab armies also moved west, invading Egypt in 639. The Byzantine rulers were not popular, and by 642 the Muslims ruled this important province. They gradually spread west into other Byzantine territories, and by 710 Muslims controlled all of North Africa.

As they conquered new lands, the Arabs offered the defeated people an opportunity to convert to Islam. This was supposed to be a free decision because Islam's holy book, the Qur'an, forbids forcible conversion. Some Africans found the new faith an attractive alternative to their old beliefs. Others converted for a more worldly reason, recognizing that as Muslims they would have greater rights in the Islamic state. Jews and Christians were permitted to keep their religions, if they wished, although they had to swear allegiance to the Muslim state and pay a special tax.

During the eighth and ninth centuries, the Muslims established outposts throughout North Africa, from which they could defend against Byzantine attacks. These outposts, called *ribats*, developed into Muslim communities, where people came to worship and to trade with others.

As with Christianity, during the first several centuries of Islamic history there was a struggle among followers of the faith in determining how religious teachings should be interpreted. Some Muslims attempted to introduce their own cultural practices and teachings, or the philosophical thought of the ancient Greeks, Romans, Persians, or other cultures, into Islamic practice. The successors of Muhammad, called caliphs, and other religious leaders actively discouraged and persecuted these dissenters, forcing them to flee to remote areas of the Islamic world.

Two sects that found their way to the sparsely populated areas of North Africa were the Shiites (followers of Ali, a relative of Muhammad) and the Kharijites (a group of Muslims that had broken away from the main faith during the seventh century). These outcasts settled in the desert mountains of the region known as the Maghreb (which includes the modern states of Algeria, Tunisia, and Morocco), where they intermarried with, and converted, the local Berber and Tuareg inhabitants. During the eighth and ninth

Islam spread gradually throughout North Africa, but by the ninth century it had become the dominant faith of the region. Muslim rulers built mosques and monuments such as the Koutoubia Mosque in Morocco, constructed during the 12th century.

This early manuscript of a verse from the Qur'an was found in North Africa.

centuries, groups of Kharijites took control of various parts of North Africa, capturing cities like Kairouan and Tlemcen.

Kharijite strength in North Africa was supplanted by the rise of the Fatamids, a Shiite group, in 909. The Fatamid dynasty emerged from northern Tunisia to conquer the Maghreb, and took over Egypt in 972. The Fatamids held North Africa until 1169, when they were supplanted by Turkish invaders. Under the Turks, most people living in the coastal areas of North Africa accepted the orthodox teachings known as Sunni Islam. The people living closer to the Sahara, however, continued to follow variant forms of the religion.

MOVEMENT OF ISLAM INTO WEST AFRICA

During the Roman era, Christianity had never been able to penetrate the vast Sahara Desert. However, not long after the Muslims conquered North Africa, the Arabs and Berbers were making trade journeys south across the Sahara. The Arabs introduced camels and other livestock to the region, thus providing transportation that allowed traders to more easily cross the desert. By the end of the eighth century, traders were bringing manufactured goods and iron tools from the populated cities of North Africa, the Middle East, and Europe into West Africa, where they were traded for gold, ivory, salt, and other valuable natural resources. This contact between Muslim traders and the indigenous peoples of West Africa also helped spread Islam south into the region.

CONVERTING AFRICANS TO ISLAM

Although all Muslims must observe specific obligations, called the five pillars of Islam, a wide variety of local beliefs and practices that do not contradict these basic Islamic teachings have been permitted. This flexibility in accepting other teachings probably evolved as a practical matter; when the Arabs emerged from the desert with their new faith, they quickly conquered a vast empire containing many different peoples. To establish and maintain control over so many diverse ethnic groups, the religion had to appeal to and accommodate the practices of the locals. Muslim clerics often used the traditional religions as a starting point for converting Africans to Islam.

"Much in Islam was compatible with traditional African religious and social customs, and much of African religion was retained in Islamized form," explains Benjamin Ray in *African Religions: Symbol, Ritual, and Community*. "To some extent, Islam was built upon the foundation of the traditional religions. Conversion was facilitated by Islam's affinity to African concepts of Supreme Being, local systems of divination, the widespread use of ritual charms, and the potency of prayer and ritual action."

Perhaps the most important similarity shared by Islam and the traditional religions is a belief in a mystical, spiritual world that cannot be seen by ordinary humans, but that exerts an influence on human behavior. In addition to believing in a Supreme Being—Allah—Muslims also recognize the existence of a variety of supernatural creatures, including angels, devils, and jinn (better known in the West as genies).

According to Islamic beliefs, angels are creatures made of light that serve

By the 11th century, Muslims could be found living throughout West Africa. In his 1068 book *Of Highways and Kingdoms*, the Spanish-Arab geographer Abu Abdullah al-Bakri wrote that there were Muslim communities in three West African kingdoms. One of these was based at Gao, a city in modern-day Mali that would later become the center of the powerful Songhay Empire. The king of Gao had converted to Islam in 1009, although most of his people still practiced their traditional religion.

Such partial religious conversions commonly occurred in Africa. Often, the ruling classes—who were responsible for the

Allah in Heaven, spending most of their time praising him; they are sometimes sent as messengers to the human world, as Gabriel was sent to Muhammad. The devils are led by an evil spirit named Iblis (corresponding to Satan in the Judeo-Christian tradition); his purpose is to tempt humans to sin, and thus separate themselves from Allah. When the world ends, Allah will cast Iblis and those who follow him into hell. Muslims do not believe Iblis is a fallen angel (as Christians and Jews believe of Satan), but an evil jinn. The jinn are creatures created from smokeless fire; like men, the jinn have souls and can be either good or bad. The activities of various jinn are referred to in the Qur'an, and stories about them have been popular in Muslim lands for centuries. Muslims believe that bad jinn go about making mischief for humans—they are believed to cause illness and personal misfortunes.

Like the followers of traditional African religions, Muslims observe many superstitions and practice certain rituals to ward off the effects of evil or malicious spirits. For example, Muslims believe that whistling can attract jinn, so in many cultures it is forbidden or frowned upon. In addition, the wearing of charms or amulets for protection from evil spirits is common in both the Muslim world and in African countries. Amulets can take many forms, including jewelry worn around the neck, ankle, finger, or wrist; scraps of paper, often containing verses from the Qur'an, or drawings; and precious gems or small worn stones. These talismans are believed to bring the wearer prosperity, protect him or her from evil spirits, help the person find love, provide safety when traveling, ensure good health, or provide many other benefits.

welfare of the entire community and who had greater exposure to people and customs of the outside world—would convert, while the ordinary peasants were less affected by the arrival of the new religion, and would retain their traditional beliefs. As a result, the traders who initially introduced Islam to West Africa were followed by Muslim religious leaders, who made direct efforts to convert local rulers to their religion. In his writings al-Bakri described how an African king was converted:

> [His] country became afflicted with drought one year following another; the inhabitants prayed for rain, sacrificing cattle till they had exterminated almost all of them, but the drought and the misery only increased. The king had as his guest a Muslim [and] to this man the king complained of the calamities that assailed him and his people. The man said: "O king, if you believed in God (who is exalted) and testified that He is One, and testified as to the prophetic Mission of Muhammad . . . and if you accepted all the religious laws of Islam, I would pray for your deliverance from your plight. . . ." Thus he continued to press the king until the latter accepted Islam and became a sincere Muslim. The man made him recite from the Quran some easy passages and taught him religious obligations and practices which no one may be excused from knowing. [Then the Muslim prayed], while the king, standing at his right side, imitated him. Thus they prayed for a part of the night, the Muslim reciting invocations and the king saying, "Amen." The dawn had just started to break when God caused abundant rain to descend upon them. So the king ordered the idols to be broken and expelled the sorcerers from his country. He and his descendants after him as well as his nobles were sincerely attached to Islam, while the common people of his kingdom remained polytheists.

Sometimes, a ruler would insist that his subjects also convert to Islam. This was the case in Takrur, a small trading state located in the Senegal Valley near present-day Mauritania. After its king became a Muslim, he forced his subjects to obey Islamic law and waged wars against neighboring Africans who did not accept Islam. "The Islamic militancy of Takrur was exceptional," writes Nehemia Levtzion in *The History of Islam in Africa*, "whereas Gao represented symbiotic relations between Islam and the traditional religion that were typical of Islam in West Africa."

Between the ninth and eleventh centuries, Muslims were also well represented in one of the greatest African kingdoms during this time—the Empire of Ghana (or Wagadou). Ghana had become wealthy through the trans-Saharan trade of gold and salt, and was the most influential state in West Africa. In his writings, al-Bakri explained that although the king was not a Muslim, he welcomed Muslim traders and employed educated Muslims at his court.

Most of the people of Ghana converted to Islam after 1076, when the capital at Koumbi Saleh was captured by the Almoravids, a Muslim-Berber group from North Africa that kept control over Ghana for a decade. Although the indigenous people of the region—the Soninke—eventually regained control over the empire, it was in decline. By 1240 the growing Empire of Mali had subsumed Ghana. But the Islamization of the Ghana Empire profoundly influenced the continuing spread of Islam throughout West Africa.

The Mali Empire dominated West Africa from the 13th to the 15th centuries. Its founder, the Mandinka chief Sundiata Keita, had converted to Islam around 1240, and his descendants were devout Muslims, building mosques and observing Islamic rituals. The most famous Muslim king of Mali was Mansa Musa, Sundiata's grandnephew, who went on a memorable *hajj* (pilgrimage to Mecca) in 1324. At the time, Mali was the source of much of the world's gold, and it was said that Mansa Musa gave away so much gold during his trip that the value of the commodity plummeted and did not recover for 12 years. More important, however, was that during his rule the Malian city of Timbuktu became renowned for Islamic studies. The university of Sankore, in Timbuktu, was famed as a center of learning throughout the Muslim world, with the largest collection of books in all of Africa. A West African proverb of the time says, "Salt comes from the north, gold from the south, but the word of God and the treasures of wisdom come from Timbuktu."

As the Mali Empire declined during the 15th century, the strongly Islamic Songhay Empire, which covered western Sudan and parts of Niger, rose in its place. The Kanem Empire to the east of the Songhay had also accepted Islam. Muslim travelers between these two empires—the Muslim Fulani tribe and Muslim clerics following trade routes—soon introduced the Hausa tribes of modern-day northern Nigeria to the Islamic culture. The Hausa developed a strong Muslim identity that continues to this day.

During the early 19th century, a man named Usman dan Fodio (1754–1817) led a Muslim uprising that established a powerful Islamic community in West Africa, and contributed to a resurgence of Islamic belief in the region. Fodio was an educated Muslim of the Fulani tribe, and he established a small community governed by Islamic law in what today is northern Nigeria. In 1802, Fodio and his followers were forced to flee from their settlement by the Hausa, who dominated West Africa at the time. In response, Fodio gained support among the Fulani and launched a Muslim uprising, or jihad ("holy war") against the Hausa. By 1810, Fodio's followers had gained control of a West African region stretching from modern-day Burkina Faso to Cameroon. This Islamic empire would become known as the

Arab travelers arrive in Timbuktu, which in the 14th century was an important center of African Islamic scholarship and religious life.

Sokoto Caliphate. It was one of the last great West African empires, lasting for nearly a century until it was undermined and destroyed by pressures of European colonialism.

ISLAM ARRIVES IN EAST AFRICA

The first Muslims who came to East Africa did not even have the name *Muslims* at the time, they were followers of Muhammad who were fleeing from persecution in Mecca. They found sanctuary in the Ethiopian kingdom of Aksum around A.D. 615.

During the seventh and early eighth centuries Muslim Arabs spread their religion into Europe, North Africa, and Asia primarily through conquest. But Islam's spread into East Africa was far more peaceful. As with the spread of the religion into West Africa, Islam was first brought to East Africa by traders and travelers during the eighth and ninth centuries. In the case of East Africa, it first appeared in ports on the Indian Ocean, from the Horn of Africa south along the coast to Mozambique, as well as on the nearby islands of Madagascar and Zanzibar. Gradually, the religion spread into the interior.

One reason that Islam spread so quickly along trade routes was because it established a framework for fair dealings. Muslim merchants were governed by a shared set of rules for moral conduct (the Sharia). In addition, the Muslims introduced writing—then unknown in sub-Saharan Africa—to indigenous traders, and also developed new methods of weighing and measuring goods. As the Muslim trading network grew, it became advantageous for African merchants and traders to convert to Islam. Over time, the language known as Swahili developed out of the need for African, Arab, and Asian traders in the Indian Ocean to be able to understand each other.

East Africans who converted to Islam realized other benefits as well. Islamic law imposed a consistent order among different

اﻟﻘ ﺮآ ن ﺛﻤ ﺮ اﺑﻌﺪ ا ﺳﺎﻃﻴﺮ ﺑﻼﻫ ﺎ و رﺣﺎ رف ﺣ ﻼﻫ ﺎ و ﻗﺎ ل ا رﻛﺒ ﻮا ﺑﻬ ﺎ ﺑﺴ ﻢ اﻟﻠ ﻪ ﻣﺤ ﺮاﻫﺎ

و ﻣ ﺮﺳﺎﻫﺎﻧ ﺖ ﺛﻤ ﺔ ﻧﻔ ﺲ ﻧﻔ ﺲ اﻟﻤﻐ ﻤ ﻤﻴ ﻦ ا و ﻋﺒﺎ د اﻟﻠ ﻪ ﻟﻠﻤﻜ ﺮﻣﻴ ﻦ و ﻗﺎ ل اﻣﺎ اﻧﺎ

This page from a 12th-century Arabic manuscript shows the traditional dhow, a sailing ship used by traders to cross the Indian Ocean. Beginning in the eighth century, seafaring traders from the Arabian Peninsula—and later, Muslim missionaries—introduced Islam to the people living in East African port cities.

societies, so the spread of religion meant that in some cases, loyalties to a particular ethnic group were replaced by loyalty to a state and its religion.

"Before long the arrival of Islam in Mombasa and coastal Tanzania affected diverse areas of the cultural experience of the people," writes Ali A. Mazrui:

> Marriage and kinship relations were changed profoundly, as were the rules of inheritance and succession. African indigenous norms were often in competition with the Islamic rules. In some cases syncretism was the result; in some cases the indigenous norms still had an edge; but increasingly the Afro-Oriental phase of Swahili history witnessed the gradual pre-colonial triumph of the Islamic rules of marriage, kinship, inheritance and succession.

For some Africans, the transition from their traditional religions to Islam was made easier because the newer religion permitted certain traditional behaviors and actions. For example, polygamy, the practice of having multiple wives, was a traditional African practice that was also viewed as acceptable within the Muslim tradition, although forbidden by Christianity. Slavery was another practice that was both accepted and common in the Muslim lands of East Africa. Although Islam prohibited the enslaving of free Muslims who lived in Islamic territories, non-Muslims from outside of the coastal region could be enslaved. Captured Africans were sold to work in the salt mines of the Sahara, in the gold mines of Nubia, or for wealthy Muslims in the Middle East. Islamic rulers in Turkey, North Africa, and the Middle East also made use of slaves in their armies.

By the 14th century, when the Arab traveler Ibn Battuta visited the region, Islam was the dominant

A busy street market in Zanzibar, circa 1912. Although the island was a British protectorate after 1890, it continued to be ruled by Muslim sultans until 1964.

religion of the East African coast. Battuta wrote about feeling at home in East Africa because of the preponderance of Muslims.

The Portuguese seafarer Vasco da Gama, who led the first expedition around the southern tip of Africa and into the Indian Ocean, arrived at Mombasa (in present-day Kenya) in 1498 on his way to India. The Gama expedition was relatively peaceful— although his men did capture Arab sailors, whom they forced to accompany them and show the best route to India. However, the Portuguese were soon back with warships, using their cannons—a weapon rarely found in East Africa at the time—to capture key ports from the Arab and African Muslims.

Portuguese influence did not last long. By the 17th century other European powers, notably the Dutch and British, had supplanted the Portuguese as the dominant sea powers in the Indian Ocean. Control over the East African coast passed to the Muslim sultans of Oman, on the Arabian Peninsula. It was during this time that Islam began to spread into the interior of Africa. Muslim clerics and missionaries encouraged tribal chiefs in places like modern-day Uganda, Rwanda, and Burundi, and in the area around Lake Tanganyika, to convert to Islam. By the time these regions fell under colonial rule during the 19th century, a growing percentage of the population was Muslim.

6 ISLAM IN AFRICA TODAY

During the 19th century, European countries like Britain, France, and Germany established colonies throughout Africa, just as they had over other areas of the world. Great Britain, for example, ruled over parts of East Africa as well as Egypt, the Sudan, and South Africa. France controlled Algeria, Morocco, and much of West Africa. Germany possessed colonies in southern Africa, while Italy, Belgium, and other European countries also maintained a colonial presence on the continent.

COLONIALISM AND THE ISLAMIC RESPONSE

The European powers used their superior weaponry and technology to destroy or undermine the existing states of sub-Saharan Africa, bringing them under their control. In Nigeria, for example, the Muslim Sokoto Caliphate crumbled, and its territories were divided among the British and French. (British leaders did give the caliphate's rulers a great deal of leeway to control the local population in Nigeria; to this day one of Usman dan Fodio's descendants still holds the position of sultan of Sokoto, the main religious leader of Nigerian Muslims.)

Muslims fought back against colonial encroachment in other parts of the continent as well. The Wassoulou Empire of West Africa, which included parts of modern-day Guinea, Mali, Sierra Leone, and Cote d'Ivoire, was established as an Islamic state in the 1870s. Its ruler, Samori Ture, took the title "Chief of all Believers" in 1884, and Africans under his rule were ordered to convert to Islam. However, during the 1880s and 1890s the French gradually expanded their colonial presence into West Africa. Ture's capture in 1898 marked the end of the Wassoulou Empire, and of effective resistance to French authority in West Africa.

In Sudan, a Muslim leader named Muhammad Ahmed declared a jihad against the British occupation in the 1880s. Muhammad Ahmed declared himself to be the Mahdi, a messianic figure that, according to some Islamic sects, will create a socially just world on Earth in accordance with Allah's teachings. In 1885, the Mahdi captured Khartoum from the British, driving them out of the country. The Mahdi and his successors then established a state based on Islamic principles. It survived until 1898, when a British army devastated the Sudanese forces at the Battle of Omdurman.

Colonialism did not just mean the end of existing states, it also sparked dramatic changes within the Muslim communities of Africa. The European powers replaced the tribal government structure with new administrations and removed religion from its once-central role in social and economic organization. In Muslim areas governed by Islamic law, or Sharia, the colonial powers instituted European legal systems. As a result, today many African countries with Muslim populations have dual legal systems, with laws governing most personal matters based on Islamic law, while most criminal and trade laws are based on European legal models.

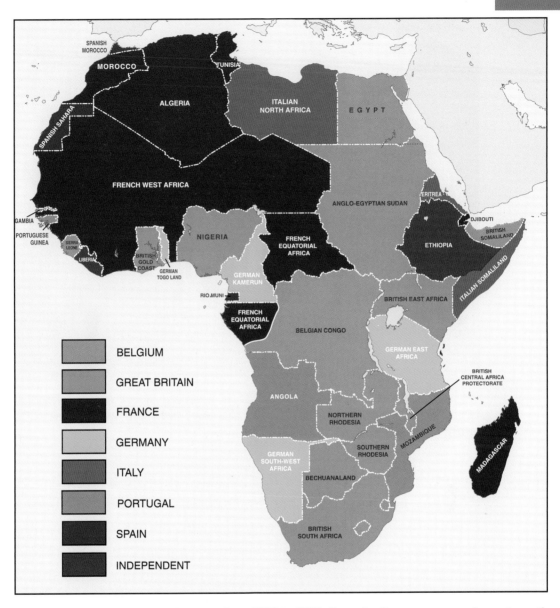

BELGIUM

GREAT BRITAIN

FRANCE

GERMANY

ITALY

PORTUGAL

SPAIN

INDEPENDENT

At a conference held in Berlin, Germany, from 1884 to 1885, the major European powers began to partition Africa among themselves. By 1914 their "Scramble for Africa" had ended with the major European powers laying claim to most of the continent.

During the colonial period, many Muslims perceived an ebb in Islamic influence throughout the world; this was especially true in the 1920s, after World War I and the collapse of the Ottoman Empire. To compensate for this loss of power, numerous movements developed in the Middle East and Asia to

The European powers exploited the resources and manpower of their African colonies. In this 1935 photo, Kenyan porters carry valuable ivory tusks that will be exported to foreign markets.

reform Islam and return it to a prominent place in society. For example, in 1928 a teacher in Egypt named Hasan al-Banna (1906–1949) started an organization called the Muslim Brotherhood. At first, its purpose was to promote morality and charitable works, but over time the Brotherhood evolved into a political organization whose members called for the replacement of secular governments in Egypt and neighboring Islamic countries with governments based on Islamic law. As such, the Brotherhood became one of the earliest Islamist groups.

Islamism is a modern political ideology in which Islam is considered not only a religion, but also a comprehensive political system. Islamists believe that Islamic laws and principles should govern all aspects of life within their state. Often, the goal of Islamists is to rid their societies of "corrupting" Western influences, and return them to a purer Islam in which Sharia is the basis of law.

ISLAMIC MOVEMENTS AFTER INDEPENDENCE

During the early 20th century, another movement, African nationalism, gained many followers. African nationalists sought political power, laboring to throw off colonial control and establishing their own independent states. By the 1930s, nationalist groups existed throughout the continent. France, Britain, and other colonial powers were economically and militarily devastated by the Second World War (1939–1945), and during the 1950s and early 1960s, there was a rising sentiment for independence among the African countries.

Muslims played an important role in the independence movements, but as the newly independent states fell under a series of corrupt and brutal dictators, many Muslims became disillusioned with their Western-style governments. Thus, in some predominantly Muslim regions during the 1980s, 1990s, and 2000, local political groups have succeeded in replacing secular laws with Sharia-based legal codes. This has often led to unrest and violence between Muslims and other groups. For example, in Sudan the imposition of an Islamic government resulted in a long-running civil war that has led to more than 2 million deaths and the displacement of many indigenous people in the southern part of the country. In northern Nigeria, where 12 of the country's 36 states have adopted Sharia as law since the late 1990s, there has been friction between Muslims and non-Muslims. The latter feel Sharia punishments—such as the severing of limbs, stoning, hanging, and flogging—are too harsh.

Some Westerners have argued that Sharia is an outdated legal system that should be changed to reflect contemporary approaches to justice and punishment. Many Muslims, however,

THE ORIGINS OF SHARIA

As Islam spread into new lands with an array of cultural and tribal practices, Islamic leaders realized an organized structure of law and ritual had to be created. New converts needed to be shown a clear path of the actions and behaviors considered acceptable or unacceptable to the Muslim community.

Most Muslims believe Muhammad laid out this path both through his teachings and through his exemplary life. The Qur'an contains Muhammad's teachings, which he received from Allah; however, specific details of proper religious or social practices had to be interpreted from the Qur'anic text, as well as from stories about Muhammad and his closest companions. These stories are known as Hadith, and during the ninth and tenth centuries scholars sifted through thousands of stories to determine which were true. Once the authoritative Hadith were determined, Muslim legal scholars could see how the original Muslim community had dealt with various issues. This would set the path for future Muslims to follow.

Muslim jurists and theologians next focused on clarifying Islam's dogmatic and theological beliefs and codifying these into a body of rules that would guide the *umma*. (Muslim scholars, jurists, and theologians who could interpret scripture and formulate dogma became known collectively as the *ulama*.) Through study of the Qur'an and the authentic Hadith, the ulama developed an inventory of acceptable and restricted behaviors and actions. This became known as Sharia (Arabic for "way"). Muslims consider Sharia an all-embracing system that should govern every aspect of Islamic life.

To create this body of law, the *ulama* used two important principles. One was reasoning by analogy (*qiyas*), by which Muslim jurists could take restrictions or permissions that are clearly defined in the Qur'an or Hadith and apply them to different situations, if there were some basis for comparison. For example, the Qur'an prohibits the consumption of wine, so jurists determined that Muslims could not drink any alcoholic beverages. The other principle used in the creation of law was the consensus of the community (*ijma*). If an issue arose that was not covered in the Qur'an or the Hadith, the leading scholars of the Muslim community could decide how to best proceed.

The process of using *qiyas* and *ijma* to interpret the holy law is called *ijtihad*. However, by the eleventh century many Muslims believed all of the important questions related to their faith had been answered. This led to a general agreement prohibiting significant changes to the law, which became known as "closing the gates of *ijtihad*." As a result, although contemporary Muslim jurists can debate the application or interpretation of existing laws, they cannot expand the laws outside the existing Sharia structure.

counter that Sharia is a moral code—one for which there are various interpretations—and explain that it is much more than its controversial punishments. "When people think about Sharia law, they often think about the penalties for certain crimes," Imam Feisal Abdul Rauf of the Masjid al-Farah mosque in New York City told the television program *Frontline* in 2003. "They don't think about the sum total of Islamic law and its jurisprudence, which means the underlying structure and philosophy and understanding of how you arrive at what we call the Islamically correct decision. You do not define Sharia law by just a couple of penalties."

THE DISTRIBUTION OF MUSLIMS IN AFRICA TODAY

In today's African countries, many of which are saddled with bad governments and high levels of poverty, Islam as both a religious and political system is attractive to many people. "It is difficult to overstate the importance of Islam as a source of identity to Africans in societies that are experiencing rapid change," write Charlotte and Frederick Quinn in *Pride, Faith, and Fear: Islam in Sub-Saharan Africa*. "To be able to say, 'I am a Muslim' is to have an identity and access to a wider community of shared beliefs, a code of behavior in the present world, and hope for the life hereafter. Believers can gain strength from the knowledge that they are part of a worldwide community (*umma*)."

Today, approximately 460 million Africans identify themselves as Muslims. About half of them live in the Arab states of North Africa: Egypt, Algeria, Morocco, Tunisia, Libya, Mauritania, and the disputed Western Sahara territory. However, Muslim communities can be found in every African country of sub-Saharan Africa, ranging in size from a few thousand (Zimbabwe) to virtually the entire population (Somalia and Senegal). The number of Muslims in Africa is expanding rapidly, due both to ongoing conversions and to the rapid population growth among Muslims.

In North Africa, Egypt contains the largest number of Muslims, with a population of more than 85 million. It is followed by Algeria (38 million), Morocco (32 million), Tunisia (10.8 million), Libya (6 million), Mauritania (3.4 million), and the Western Sahara (about 540,000). In Sudan, to the south of Egypt, most of the country's 34 million people are followers of Islam. Islam is the state religion and Sharia the basis for laws in Sudan.

Many countries of East Africa have significant Muslim populations, including Ethiopia (33 million), Tanzania (12.6 million), Somalia (more than 8 million), and Uganda (4.1 million). The Muslim population of Kenya is not known for certain; estimates range from 3.2 million to nearly 8 million. Other countries with large Muslim communities are Malawi (2.3 million), Eritrea (2.2 million), Madagascar (1.2 million), and Djibouti (432,000).

In central Africa, Chad has a large Muslim community of over 5.8 million, more than half of the country's total population. Other countries of central Africa that have significant Muslim communities include the Democratic Republic of the Congo (5.6 million), Cameroon (3.15 million), Central African Republic (550,000), and Rwanda (360,000).

Islam is the major religion of West Africa. In Nigeria, the most populous country of Africa with more than 170 million people, about half are Muslims. As a result, Nigeria is the home of the majority of sub-Saharan Muslims.

Muslims also make up the majority in the West African countries of Burkina Faso (10.4 million Muslims, or 60 percent of the total population), the Gambia (1.66 million; 90 percent of the population), Guinea (9.25 million; 85 percent of the population), Mali (14.7 million; 95 percent of the population), Niger (13 million; 80 percent of the population), Senegal (12.2 million; 94

Nigeria has the largest Muslim population of sub-Saharan Africa, with approximately 85 million Muslims. These Nigerian women are participating in a prayer service in a mosque in Lagos.

percent of the population), and Sierra Leone (3.2 million; about 60 percent of the population). There are also Muslim communities of significant size in Benin, Cote d'Ivoire, Ghana, Liberia, and Togo.

In the countries of southern Africa, which were British colonies for many years, Muslim communities are smaller. Zambia has about 3 million Muslims, or nearly a quarter of that country's total population. In contrast, the proportion of Muslims in South Africa—the region's most populous nation with 48.8 million people—is around 1.5 percent.

7 RELIGIOUS CONFLICTS IN AFRICA

hen the colonial powers divided up the continent at the 1884–85 Berlin Conference, they drew new political boundaries in Africa that reflected European interests and demands. But these boundaries did not take into account where various ethnic or religious groups lived, or the traditional trade and social relationships among Africa's peoples. Thus, in many cases the new colonies were home to several ethnic or religious groups that traditionally had been rivals or enemies. Under colonialism, European powers imposed control over these groups and most Africans were tolerant of other belief systems. Religion rarely played a major role in the continent's various conflicts.

During the post-colonial period, however, religion became a more divisive issue. When the colonial powers granted independence to their former colonies during the 1960s and 1970s, the colonial borders—created without the input of the Africans who lived within them—became the borders of African states. In Nigeria, for example, there are around 300 ethnic groups; the largest of these include the Hausa and Fulani (which are predominantly Muslim), the Yoruba (most of whom are either Pentecostal Christian or practice indigenous religions), and the Igbo (who are predominantly Catholic).

Throughout Africa authoritarian leaders have sometimes used religious differences to create a wedge between ethnic groups in order to better maintain control. Frequently, such leaders would favor their own religious community at the expense of others, thereby alienating some communities and creating resentment and tension. In these countries, it was not religion per se that caused the conflict, but religion became the identifying characteristic delineating sides. In the civil wars in Nigeria (1967–1970) and Sudan (1983–2003), Christian-Muslim animosity exacerbated tensions related to political and economic disparity among ethnic or regional groups.

MUSLIM-CHRISTIAN TENSIONS IN NIGERIA

Before the arrival of European settlers, the Hausa, Yoruba, and Igbo tribes in the area now called Nigeria were separate and often hostile toward one another. They differed in almost every possible respect, including language, tradition, religious practice, and ethnicity. Unlike the predominantly Muslim Hausa, who lived in highly organized societies, the Igbo lived in mostly isolated villages ruled by direct democracy. They had no kings. And the Igbo as an ethnic group had no tribal leader. This group had little interaction with the Hausa in the north until the British created the colony of Nigeria. The stark differences between the tribes were noted by Sir Hugh Clifford, the colony's first governor-general.

At first, Nigeria was governed under two administrative bodies, the Protectorate of Northern Nigeria and the Protectorate of

Southern Nigeria. As it became increasingly clear to the Igbo that they had nothing in common with the Muslim Hausa, a sense of tribal unity began to develop. The Igbo adopted Christianity and attended mission schools, making them even more distinct from the northern tribe, while also gaining them favor with the ruling British.

In 1922, the two Nigerian protectorates were merged under a new constitution that split the country into four regions: Northern Province (Hausa), Western Province (Yoruba), Eastern Province (Igbo), and the colony of Lagos. These political divisions only reinforced the division between the Hausa and the Igbo, as now they had a single government over which to vie for control. As Nigeria moved toward independence, it became clear that each province wanted strong regional control with almost no central government. When the British granted independence in 1960, Nigeria was left with four political entities only loosely cobbled together by a federal constitution.

From 1960 to 1965, an Igbo-Hausa alliance ruled the country at the expense of the Yoruba. In 1965, however, a new Yoruba political movement formed an alliance with fellow Muslim Hausa in the north and won a majority in national elections that year, though fraud was rampant at the polls. The ousted Igbo joined with the Christian Yoruba to form an opposition party.

Fearing marginalization of their ethnic group, Igbo officers in the military overthrew Nigeria's government in January 1966. However, a counter coup by the northerners in July 1966 forced the Igbo from power. The Igbo living in the northern part of the country were victims of massacres at the hands of Muslims. In an attempt to calm the situation, the government moved all Igbo soldiers from their stations around the country to stations within the Eastern Province. (The ethnic mixture in the military had been the last vestige of the ideal of a unified Nigeria.) The Igbo in the south declared their independence on May 30, 1967, as a new Christian-majority nation, the Republic of Biafra.

Because much of Nigeria's oil reserves were in the southern areas now claimed by Biafra, the Nigerian government immediately responded to the declaration of secession by invading the province. To encourage conscription among the people in the north and west, Nigeria began a propaganda campaign centered on the idea of national unity, even though unity had never really been a goal for any of the provinces.

Throughout 1967 the armies of both sides won and lost cities, with the Biafrans finally being driven back into their own region. Unable to win through direct assault, the Nigerians settled into siege. Their navy blockaded Biafra's ports and took control of two

Nigerian rebels watch for enemy troops during the 1967–70 civil war in Biafra. The conflict, in which a predominantly Christian region attempted to break away from the Muslim-dominated government in Nigeria, was among the most brutal in Africa's history.

port towns: Bonny and Calabar. Biafra had to import goods and weapons in order to support its military, so with the flow of goods cut off, it soon no longer had the resources with which to fight. The Nigerian army destroyed Biafran farmland, cutting off the only source of food for the fledgling republic and causing mass starvation.

Nigeria's civil war, which lasted until 1970, was one of the first civil wars in post-independence Africa and also one of the bloodiest. It is estimated that over a million people died from fighting, disease, or starvation. The brutal nature of the blockade—which led to mass starvation and disease—attracted the sympathy of the world, and the Nigerian government was accused of gross human rights abuses. The international organization Doctor Without Borders was founded as a response to the Red Cross's inability to help the Igbo during the siege. While the conflict had multiple factors (as is the case with all civil wars), religious tensions between the country's Muslims and Christians played an important role.

ONGOING TENSIONS IN NIGERIA

The end of the civil war did not eliminate religious and ethnic tensions in Nigeria, though. During the 1970s and 1980s the military continued to have a strong influence over the government, and power changed hands several times through coups. In 1999, Olusegun Obasanjo was elected president of Nigeria and a new constitution was instated. Although the country returned to civilian rule in 1999, hundreds of people are still killed each year in clashes between Muslims and Christians.

One factor that has contributed to the tension is the implementation of Sharia courts in 12 of Nigeria's northern provinces, where large numbers of Muslims live. These courts apply strict penalties to those who transgress against Islamic law; for example, the hands of thieves are cut off and those caught being drunk in public are caned. Supporters of the courts say the harsh penalties help reduce crime, but many non-Muslims believe that the laws are outdated and unfair, and some Christians feel they create an atmosphere of intimidation and encourage violence against non-Muslims. Sanctioned vigilante groups enforcing Sharia among the populace have become common.

In 2002, radical Islamic fundamentalism fueled violence that caused the deaths of over 100 people in the town of Kaduna. The Miss World beauty pageant was supposed to take place in Nigeria, but after a newspaper article stated that the Prophet Muhammad would approve of the pageant, angry Muslims started burning Christian churches and murdering townspeople. Some men were burned alive.

In 2004, more than 1,000 people were killed in fighting between Christians and Muslims. And further violence occurred in early 2006, when angry Nigerian Muslims used the publication of cartoons considered offensive to Islam as an excuse to riot in several northern cities, attacking and killing Christians and burning churches. In the south, Nigerian Christians responded by burning mosques and Muslim-owned shops and killing Muslims.

In early 2010, the central Nigerian city of Jos became the focus of renewed Muslim-Christian violence, which Christian farmers of the Berom ethnic group clashign with ethnic Fulani herdsmen who practice Islam. A series of attacks by machete-wielding mobs left nearly 1,000 people dead.

While religion provided a convenient dividing line between populations that differ ethnically, culturally, and—perhaps most important—economically in Nigeria, during the civil war religious doctrine has come to take a more prominent place in the conflict. There remains an economic divide that is difficult to discount, but Sharia law and Islamism have introduced a new level of proselytizing that was unseen during the civil war. The

Nigerians look at a mosque damaged by rioting Christians in Onitsha, February 2006. In the past two decades, fighting fueled by religious differences and encouraged by both Christian and Muslim extremists has become all too common in Nigeria.

application of Sharia affects the conflict in a way that previous fighting had not.

THE SUDANESE CIVIL WAR

Sudan, Africa's second-largest country in terms of land area, has been torn by civil war for nearly all of its existence as an independent nation. Northern Sudan is predominantly Muslim in religion and Arab in ethnicity. Southern Sudan is non-Arab and non-Muslim; the people who live in the south are ethnically more closely related to African groups in Kenya and Tanzania, and practice either Christianity or traditional African religions. However, although religious differences have played a part in Sudan's history of civil war, many other factors have contributed to unrest in the country. The struggle for economic resources is a major factor: oil, one of Sudan's most valuable natural commodities, is located in the south, as are the country's most fertile agricultural lands.

On gaining independence from Great Britain in 1956, Sudan formed a predominantly Arab and Muslim government in Khartoum. The new government immediately faced an insurgency from the Christian south that lasted until 1972 and led to over 500,000 deaths. Attempts by the Sudanese government to impose Islamic culture on the south only bolstered the rebellion. The accord that ended the civil war broke down in 1983, when the government attempted to establish Sharia as the basis for Sudan's national laws. Christians in the south who did not want to be subject to Islamic law launched a second war. This conflict between the government and the Sudanese People's Liberation Army (SPLA) raged for over 20 years. Millions of Sudanese were killed by fighting, starvation, and disease; millions more became homeless refugees.

A feeling of exhaustion among the Sudanese people, along with pressure from the international community, led to a cease-fire in 2003. A peace agreement between the government and the SPLA was signed in January 2005. Under the terms of the agreement, southern Sudan was autonomous for six years. During this time, revenues from the south's oil fields were to be split 50-50 between the southerners and the government in Khartoum.

In January 2011, the people of South Sudan voted overwhelmingly in favor of secession from Sudan. The Republic of South Sudan became independent on July 9, 2011.

The war in Sudan is an instance in which the religious aspects exacerbated a situation that was essentially an economic and ethnic divide. Because Sudan had such a disparate population, the attempt by northerners to forcefully convert people in the south only served to promote animosity.

A Catholic priest performs mass at a camp for Sudanese refugees, 1989. It is estimated that Sudan's long-running conflict, which pitted the Muslim-dominated government in Khartoum against Christian and animist rebels in the South, resulted in nearly 2 million deaths. Another 4 million Sudanese were forced to leave their homes because of the fighting.

In some other African states, however, religion itself has been a major factor in civil war. In Algeria, the 1992–2002 civil war was an aspect of the larger global struggle taking place in the Muslim world between Islamists, who believe religious laws and beliefs should be the basis of government, and those who prefer a secular approach to government.

RELIGIOUS FUNDAMENTALISM IN ALGERIA

After a brutal eight-year-long war in which nearly a million Algerians died, Algeria achieved independence from France in 1962. For the next 30 years, a single political party, the National Liberation Front (*Front de Libération Nationale*, or FLN), controlled Algeria. By the late 1980s, however, many Algerians were frustrated with FLN's heavy-handed rule. Most people were poor, despite the fact that Algeria controls significant amounts of oil and natural gas resources.

Algeria is a predominantly Muslim nation—by law, the president is required to be Muslim—but the FLN had governed as a secular, socialist party. Under the new constitution adopted in 1989 that allows multiple parties, a religious opposition party called the Islamic Salvation Front (*Front Islamique du Salut*, or FIS) developed. Leaders of this party expressed a variety of goals, from the moderate to the extreme; however, the main goal of the FIS was to establish an Islamic state governed by laws that are compatible with Sharia law.

In the country's first multiparty parliamentary election, held in 1991, the Islamic Salvation Front stunned the FLN by winning many seats in the new parliament. Before the next elections could take place in 1992, the Algerian military (which was controlled by the FLN) seized control of the government, cancelled the elections, and banned the FIS.

Algeria quickly descended into civil war, as armed FIS militias fought the Algerian army. More radical and violent groups, including the Armed Islamic Group (GIA), joined with the FIS and attempted to destabilize the military government by committing terrorist attacks in Algeria's cities and massacring civilians in the countryside. The radical group justified its actions on the basis that Algerians would either see the light and truth of the GIA's "holy goal" of establishing an Islamic fundamentalist state or be put to death. The government-controlled military matched this brutality, killing thousands of Algerians—mostly civilians—in an effort to destroy the Islamist movement. However, in the mid-1990s a split developed among the Islamist parties, and the GIA turned on the Islamic Salvation Front's militia, the Islamic Salvation Army (AIS).

In battles with both the AIS and the Algerian army, the GIA began massacring civilians and burning entire villages in an effort to spread terror and fear across the country. In 1997, the AIS capitulated and requested a cease-fire. The GIA eventually fell apart from the inside due to disagreements among its members over its brutal policy of razing villages.

The war gradually ended after Algerians returned to the polls in the late 1990s to vote for a new president. Although the Islamist groups boycotted the elections and declared them to be

Fresh graves stand in a cemetery in Algeria in 1997, at the height of that country's brutal civil war.

fraudulent, they produced a president—Abdelaziz Bouteflika—in 1999. The following year the FIS disbanded its armed militia, and many combatants accepted the terms of a new amnesty program. The GIA had been practically destroyed by 2002; however, occasionally violence still erupts between the Algerian army and more radical Islamic groups. Approximately 100,000 Algerians died during the eight years of civil war, and the country's economy and society were shattered.

CHAOS IN SOMALIA

In 1991, with the fall of dictator General Mohamed Siad Barre, Somalia became a failed state. Without a viable central government, the country broke apart. The northern section declared its independence, calling itself Somaliland. Meanwhile, the military strongmen, or warlords, who drove Barre out of power began opposing one another for control of the country. Widespread fighting, political chaos, and starvation in Somalia led the United Nations in 1992 to authorize a Unified Task Force (Unitaf) to enter the country and make it safe for humanitarian relief operations. Unitaf was led by the U.S. military and included troops from many other nations, including France, Belgium, Canada, Italy, Pakistan, and Nigeria.

The UN mandate in Somalia changed in 1993 to include disarming warlords' militias and establishing a new government. At that time many of the Somali warlords signed a cease-fire resolution and promised to be part of a new unity government. However, one warlord, General Mohammed Farrah Aidid, resisted, and fighting resumed in the city of Mogadishu. Aidid's men attacked UN peacekeepers, and in turn the UN issued an order for Aidid's arrest. After a U.S. operation against Aidid failed, American troops withdrew from Somalia in 1994. The following year the United Nations left as well, although order in the country had not been restored.

The lack of a government in Somalia led some Islamic groups to set up Sharia courts in parts of Mogadishu. These Islamic courts, policed by their own militias, were established in 1993 in northern Mogadishu, and a year later in southern and western parts of the city. Through these judicial systems, criminals were arrested, prosecuted, and punished according to Sharia law. Later, the Islamic courts began providing other kinds of services to the community, including healthcare and police patrols. The secular warlords in control of Mogadishu took issue with the Islamic courts, which by 2006 had formed a coalition calling itself the Supreme Council of Islamic Courts, or the Islamic Courts Union (ICU).

That June the ICU, led by Sheikh Hassan Dahir Aweys, captured Mogadishu from the warlords. The Islamists also seized the city of Jowhar, and gained control over land to the south, establishing control over the country's major ports. After living with violence on their streets for more than 16 years, the Somalis in Mogadishu were grateful for the peace that the ICU government brought. Many Somalis regarded the group as the country's new legitimate government. However, other nations had already recognized a secular Somali government, the Transitional Federal Government, which in 2005 had been established in western Somalia, in the town of Baidoa.

With the support of Ethiopian troops, the Transitional Federal Government eliminated the ICU's influence over much of Somalia by early 2007. Moderate ICU members joined the Transitional Federal Government (a moderate Islamist, Sheikh Sharif Sheikh Ahmed, became president of Somalia in 2008), but

A contingent of soldiers sent by the African Union patrol a street in Kismayo, a city in southern Somalia, during October 2012. The peacekeeping troops have been in the country since the mid-2000s to help Somalia's new government maintain stability.

hardline supporters formed new insurgency groups, the largest of which called itself al-Shabaab. In 2009 the government declared that Sharia would become the basis for the Somali judicial system when a new government was implemented. In the meantime, hundreds of civilians died in power struggles with warlords and insurgents. In 2012, the Transitional Federal Government was replaced by a newly elected Federal Parliament of Somalia.

Leaders of the United States remain concerned that instability in Somalia will provide a safe haven for radical terrorist groups like al-Qaeda. World leaders have called on all factions in Somalia to share power and create a more stable and peaceful country.

TERRORISM IN AFRICA

The 20th century saw a rise in terrorist activity committed by radical Islamic organizations. In the 1950s, the Egyptian government banned the Muslim Brotherhood as a terrorist organization, and many of its leaders were arrested and executed. In 1981, Egyptian president Anwar Sadat was assassinated by disgruntled members of the group Islamic Jihad, a splinter group from the Muslim Brotherhood. Members of Islamic Jihad were angry that Sadat had made peace with Israel in 1978, that he was aligning Egypt with Western nations like the United States, and that his government was strictly secular.

During the 1990s Islamist groups hoping to upset Egypt's tourist industry launched several terrorist attacks. In 1992, the Islamist organization Gama'a al-Islamiya declared that it would attack tourists in Egypt, and since then there have been numerous shootings and bombings. Tour buses have been destroyed by bombs and gunfire, and cruise ships have been fired upon. In 2004, the Egyptian resort towns of Taba and Ras Shitan were bombed, and in 2005 the Red Sea resort of Sharm el-Sheikh, a popular tourist spot for Israelis, was hit by multiple bombs. An

U.S. Secretary of Defense William Cohen briefs reporters on an August 1998 military strike against a suspected terrorist facility in Sudan. The attack was launched in response to al-Qaeda attacks on the U.S. embassies in Kenya and Tanzania earlier that month. International terrorist organizations like al-Qaeda often thrive within weak or failed states like Somalia or Sudan, which sheltered Osama bin Laden during the early 1990s.

attack on the resort town of Dahab in 2006 resulted in the deaths of 20 people.

A series of suicide bombings in Casablanca, Morocco, during May 2003 were similarly targeted at Westerners and Israelis. Many of the targets hit were Jewish-owned businesses or Jewish cultural centers.

More recently, in 2009 a Nigerian Islamist organization calling itself Boko Haram began launching terrorist attacks. The organization's goal is to establish Sharia law throughout the country. Attacks by Boko Haram are believed to have killed more than 450 people in 2011 and over 600 in 2012. The targets are not only Christians; Muslims who accept western teachings and social practices have also been targeted.

Socialists and experts on the Middle East point out that Israel and the West are convenient targets for radical Islamic fundamentalists. There is a great disparity between societies like the United States, Great Britain, and Israel, in which many people enjoy a comfortable lifestyle, and the failing states of Africa and the Arab world. The lack of progress and prosperity creates a sense of jealousy, which can be tapped into by Islamic fundamentalists to fuel long-standing animosities.

In a paper published in the *African Security Review*, Stefan Mair points out that in those African countries that have experienced a rise in Islamic fundamentalism, the Muslim population is also the population that is the poorest and the least politically empowered. The greatest terror threat, he notes, lies in the nations where Muslims are the poor minority.

Many groups from outside Africa, such as al-Qaeda, have operated in countries of the continent, where they have attempted to tap into the frustration and anger of Muslims. In 1998, al-Qaeda cells detonated deadly bombs at the U.S. embassies in Nairobi, Kenya, and in Dar es Salaam, Tanzania. In the past, corrupt African governments have given terrorists shelter in their countries. However, since the September 11, 2001, terrorist attack on the United States, countries like Sudan and Libya, once considered state sponsors of terrorism, have largely given up these activities under pressure from the United States. And in an effort to prevent terrorism on the continent, the United States has worked in recent years to help the countries of Niger, Senegal, Nigeria, Algeria, Chad, Mali, Mauritania, Morocco, and Tunisia train their militaries in anti-terrorism tactics.

Glossary

ANIMISM—a belief in which all things in nature are believed to have conscious spirits.

AUTONOMOUS—self-sufficient; existing and functioning independently.

CALIPH—the successor to Muhammad, who serves as leader of the Islamic community.

CATECHISTS—those who teach Christian doctrine.

CHARISMATIC—used to describe Christian worship; characterized by a quest for inspired and ecstatic experiences such as healing, prophecy, and speaking in tongues.

DOGMA—a belief or a set of beliefs that a religion holds to be true.

ECUMENICAL—representing the whole of a body of churches.

EVANGELISM—the spread of Christianity, particularly through the work of people who travel to various places preaching the Gospel and teaching others about Jesus Christ.

FETISHISM—a belief that objects can have magical powers that help or protect their owner.

FUNDAMENTALISTS—people devoted to a strict and literal interpretation of their belief system.

HERESY—opinion that contradicts or deviates from accepted conventions and beliefs.

JIHAD—holy war waged in the name of Islam.

MONOTHEISTIC—relating to a belief in, or worship of, a single, all-powerful God.

ORTHODOX—conforming to or believing in traditional standards, especially in religion.

PENTECOSTAL—a classification of evangelical Christian faith communities that emphasize the power of the Holy Spirit working within the individual.

POLYGAMY—marriage to more than one wife.

POLYTHEISTIC—relating to a belief in, or worship of, multiple gods.

PROSELYTIZE—to try to win converts to one's religious faith.

SACRAMENT—a Christian rite that confers divine grace on the recipient.

SCRIPTURE—a body of writings considered sacred or authoritative by adherents of a particular religion.

SECULAR—not concerned with the religious, spiritual, or sacred.

SOCIALIST—part of a political movement advocating government involvement in the production and distribution of goods and services.

SYNCRETISTIC—the combination of different beliefs or practices

THEOLOGIAN—a specialist in theology, which is the study of religious faith, practice, and experience, especially the study of God and God's relationship to the universe.

UMMA—the worldwide community of Muslims.

Further Reading

Isichei, Elizabeth. *A History of Christianity in Africa*. Grand Rapids, Mich.: William B. Eerdmans Publishing Company, 1995.

Kavanaugh, Dorothy. *The Muslim World: An Overview*. Philadelphia: Mason Crest, 2010.

Matthews, Warren. *World Religions*. Belmont, Calif.: Wadsworth, 2012.

Mbiti, John S. *African Religions and Philosophy*. 2nd ed. New York: Heinemann, 1990.

Moseley, William. *Taking Sides: Clashing Views on African Issues*. New York: McGraw Hill, 2011.

Quinn, Charlotte A., and Frederick Quinn. *Pride, Faith, and Fear: Islam in Sub-Saharan Africa*. New York: Oxford University Press, 2003.

Ray, Benjamin C. *African Religions: Symbols, Ritual, and Community*. 2nd ed. Upper Saddle River, N.J.: Prentice Hall, 2000.

Shillington, Kevin. *History of Africa*. New York: Palgrave Macmillan, 2012.

Soares, Benjamin F., and Rene Otayek, eds. *Islam and Muslim Politics in Africa*. New York: Palgrave Macmillan, 2007.

Internet Resources

HTTP://WWW.AFRIKAWORLD.NET/AFREL

This website collects links to essays and other websites providing information on the African Traditional Religion.

HTTP://LIBRARY.STANFORD.EDU/AFRICA/RELIGION/
AFRICAN-TRADITIONAL-RELIGION.HTML

A page maintained by the religion department at Stanford University, with links to essays about the African Traditional Religion.

HTTP://WWW.ARCHES.UGA.EDU/~GODLAS/ISLAMWEST.HTML

This comprehensive page includes essays and links to online sources on Islamic history, culture, sects, law, scripture, and contemporary issues.

HTTP://WWW.NEWADVENT.ORG/CATHEN

The *Catholic Encyclopedia*, which was originally published early in the 20th century, is a searchable database of articles about important people and events in the history of Christianity.

HTTP://WWW.RATIONALCHRISTIANITY.NET

This webpage provides basic information about Christianity, and answers some of the most common questions about the religion.

Index

Numbers in **bold italic** refer to captions.

Picture Credits

Contributors

PROFESSOR ROBERT I. ROTBERG currently holds the Fulbright Research Chair in Political Development at the Balsillie School of International Affairs in Waterloo, Canada. Prior to this, from 1999 to 2010 he served as director of the Program on Intrastate Conflict and Conflict Resolution at the Kennedy School, Harvard University. He is the author of a number of books and articles on Africa, including *Transformative Political Leadership: Making a Difference in the Developing World* (2012) and *"Worst of the Worst": Dealing with Repressive and Rogue Nations* (2007). Professor Rotberg is president emeritus of the World Peace Foundation.

DR. VICTOR OJAKOROTU is head of the Department of Politics and International Relations at North-West University in Mafikeng, South Africa. He earned his Ph.D. from the University of the Witwatersrand, Johannesburg, in 2007, and has published numerous articles on African politics and environmental issues. North-West University is one of the largest institutions of higher education in South Africa, with 64,000 students enrolled at three campuses.

LORA FRIEDENTHAL graduated from Gettysburg College with a bachelor's degree in English and a minor in philosophy. This is her first book.

DOROTHY KAVANAUGH is a freelance writer who lives near Philadelphia. She holds a bachelors' degree in elementary education from Bryn Mawr College. She has written numerous books for young adults, including *The Muslim World: An Overview* (Mason Crest, 2010).